Class
War

Class
War

CHRIS WOODHEAD

LITTLE, BROWN

A *Little, Brown* Book

First published in Great Britain in 2002
by Little, Brown

A CIP catalogue record for this book
is available from the British Library.

Typeset in Berkeley by M Rules
Printed and bound in Great Britain by
Clays Ltd, St Ives plc

Little, Brown
An imprint of
Time Warner Books UK
Brettenham House
Lancaster Place
London WC2E 7EN

www.TimeWarnerBooks.co.uk

He read each wound, each weakness clear;
And struck his finger on the place,
And said: Thou ailest here, and here!

Matthew Arnold, *Memorial Verses*

Wherever there is an absence of explicit focus and definite goals – that is, wherever there is an absence of traditional 'schooling' – there is also an absence of secure and universal learning.

E. D. Hirsch Junior, *The Schools We Need*

I believe that the only way to make a major improvement in our educational system is through privatisation to the point at which a substantial fraction of all educational services is rendered to individuals by private enterprises. Nothing else will destroy or even greatly weaken the power of the current educational establishment – a necessary pre-condition for radical improvement in our education system. And nothing else will provide the public schools with the competition that will force them to improve in order to hold on to their clientele.

Milton Friedman, *Washington Post*, 19 February 1995

Contents

	Abbreviations	ix
	Introduction	1
CHAPTER 1	Standards	9
CHAPTER 2	The Lunacy of Learnacy	41
CHAPTER 3	Teachers and Teaching	67
CHAPTER 4	OFSTED	94
CHAPTER 5	Local Education Authorities	118
CHAPTER 6	Universities	136
CHAPTER 7	The Way Forward	158
	Afterword	203
	Notes	209

Abbreviations

A level	GCE Advanced Level
DfES	Department for Education and Skills
GCSE	General Certificate of Secondary Education
GTC	General Teaching Council
HNC	Higher National Certificate
HND	Higher National Diploma
ICT	Information and Communication Technology
LEAs	Local education authorities
NASUWT	National Association of Schoolmasters and Union of Women Teachers
NCSL	National College for School Leadership
NLS	National Literacy Strategy
NNS	National Numeracy Strategy
NUT	National Union of Teachers
NVQ	National Vocational Qualification
OFSTED	Office for Standards in Education
QCA	Qualifications and Curriculum Authority
RSA	Royal Society of Arts
SEU	Standards and Effectiveness Unit

Class
War

Introduction

It was one of the meetings that sticks most vividly in my mind. I was talking to a group of teachers about inspection. They listened, but only just. A young woman stood up. 'It is not us you should be criticising', she said. 'We are the product of the system. What were we told to do at college? What do our local education authority (LEA) advisers tell us to do now? Some of us have headteachers who have either given up or who are so stuck in their ways that they refuse even to begin to question current practice. And what, too, about the politicians? Are you convinced that they know what they are doing? That they understand what is really going on in schools? The day-to-day realities of our working lives?' She paused. 'Yes, of course, some teachers are no good. Some schools are failing. But it is no good you standing there blaming us. It is the elders of the tribe that you should be challenging'.

'The elders of the tribe': it is a curious way, perhaps, of putting it, but this London teacher had a very real point. Education is a tribe and its elders – the academic, administrative and political chiefs – bear a great deal of responsibility for what has happened to our schools. I cannot remember what I said in reply, but I know that it was inadequate. This book is an attempt at a better answer.

It is inevitably a complex and controversial story. In the end everything does, of course, depend upon the individual teacher in his or her classroom. Good teachers, as every parent knows, are worth their weight in gold. They are inspirational. Think back to your own childhood. Reflect for a moment on the teachers you can still, after however many years, remember. Some will stick in your mind because they brought the subject alive. You may not have been very good at it, but because this teacher was an enthusiast, because he expected you to make progress, and because – surprise, surprise – he knew how to make you sit up and listen and could explain things clearly, you were captivated. On the other hand, you can probably remember teachers who terrified you, or spent period after period dictating notes, or did not have the faintest idea how to establish a modicum of order. It is the individual teacher who, for better or worse, makes the difference. I am certain that my adult reluctance ever to set foot on a dance floor stems from the unspeakable trauma I experienced as a thirteen-year-old when I was told that I was 'unbelievably deplorable' at Highland Dancing.

The influence of the educational tribe on the individual teacher is nonetheless strong and its responsibility, therefore, real. As a student, young teachers are socialised into its ways by lecturers who have their own often very particular views on the nature of education and the craft of the classroom, and who tend to be critical of much that the last Conservative and present Labour Government have tried to achieve. They read, perhaps, books about education written by these academics. They may flip through the pages of the *Times Educational Supplement*, the trade journal that, with depressing predictability, attacks any idea or initiative that challenges the professional status quo.

No, that is wrong. It is not the 'professional' status quo. It is not professional at all. What I am talking about here is what former US Education Secretary, William Bennett, called 'The Blob'. The Blob, in England as in America, is the tribe at its unreconstructed worst: Department for Education and Skills (DfES) bureaucrats who long ago went native, local education authority politicians and officials, academics in university Departments of Education, and last but certainly not least, the teacher unions. 'Many good-hearted individuals make up', as Robert Holland has recognised, 'this huge complex, and some even say sensible things on occasion'. But collectively The Blob resists change. It is 'an entity that defends its turf with the tenacity of a wolverine, yet is as slippery and hard for reformers to wrestle down as a greased cow in a swamp'. I can only say, as one who has on many occasions tried to discuss educational matters with Doug MacAvoy, General Secretary of the National Union of Teachers, that Mr Holland's use of language is admirably precise.

Neither is it simply the elders of the tribe. For good or ill, a young teacher's immediate colleagues can exert enormous influence. Personally, I was extremely fortunate. Back in September 1969 there were four or five exceptional teachers at Priory Boys' School, Shrewsbury. Wise, humane and tolerant of my idealistic enthusiasms, they had a profound influence on my thinking about education.

Others are not so lucky. 'I'm utterly fed up', one young teacher said to me last week. She had just finished her first year in an inner-city primary school. The teacher in the next door classroom, with whom she was meant to plan work, had been at the school twenty years. He did nothing but moan. Everything was too much trouble. The kids were awful and their parents were worse. The headteacher never backed him up. The Authority was useless and the workload impossible. 'In fact', she told me, 'he never planned anything. Every Monday morning was the same. He would sidle up, deliver his usual catalogue of woe, and ask what I was going to do with my children over the coming week'. She is a strong-minded woman who had always wanted to teach and was not going to let this particular individual blacken her view of the whole profession. Teaching inner-city children is not the easiest of occupations and the whinge culture does not help. The will and enthusiasm of the most determined can be sapped all too quickly if they have the misfortune to teach in the wrong school.

The weaker the headteacher, the more likely it is that the morale of the teachers will be low. Leadership matters, and effective leadership, in education, as in every other walk of life, is in short supply. Many heads, of course, do a brilliant job. They have their finger on the pulse of what is happening in the classrooms of their schools. They have a vision of where they want the school to go and the intelligence to plot the journey that needs to be travelled. Their staff know that they are part of a successful enterprise and, not surprisingly, they feel good about themselves. But in the school year 1999–2000 inspectors judged leadership and management to be 'weak' in one in ten or nearly two and a half thousand schools. This is a damning, and extremely significant, statistic.

In public, the tribe, understandably enough, will wriggle. Its spokesmen, aided and abetted by liberal commentators determined to portray the teaching profession as a deeply oppressed minority, will do their best to deny commonsense truths about inadequate teachers and headteachers. If standards are too low, then it is because politicians have imposed too many half-baked initiatives on the profession. It is because the English despise education. It is because we are not prepared to pay the higher taxes that are needed if schools are to be funded at a reasonable level. It is because when it comes to the crunch, parents side with their children against the school. It is because the moral certainties have collapsed, leaving teachers struggling to instil some rudimentary sense of right and wrong in their increasingly alienated pupils. It is because OFSTED, under my sadistic leadership, set out to pillory and humiliate each and every teacher in schools across the land.

I do not, you will be surprised to hear, find this latter accusation entirely persuasive. You only have to sample a few inspection reports to see that OFSTED inspectors are extremely keen to celebrate every success they can find. Indeed, the squeals of union indignation that marked my time as Chief Inspector said more about the defensiveness of the more insecure and incompetent within the teaching profession than they did about the malice of the inspection process.

More of OFSTED later. The other arguments cannot be dismissed so easily. I resigned as Chief Inspector partly because I could no longer stomach the fact that millions of pounds of taxpayers' money were being wasted on misconceived initiatives that added to the bureaucratic burdens and distracted teachers and headteachers from their proper responsibilities. Extra money is never in itself the answer, but resources do matter. Good teachers deserve significantly better pay, and, if they do not get it, they will continue to leave the profession. Too many parents have too little respect for the teachers who, against all the odds, are trying to teach their unpromising offspring. We do tend to believe that schools can solve the myriad of social ills that affect our society and many of us are too ready to believe that the collapse of western civilisation as we know it is entirely down to the inability of teachers to teach. We no longer trust our politicians enough to bother to vote? Let's introduce a period or two of Citizenship into the National Curriculum. That will reverse the cynicism and restore a belief in the democratic ideal.

If only it were that simple. If only, as many teachers justifiably complain, politicians accepted that they might be responsible for some at least of our social and economic problems. If only they understood that when you expect teachers to do more and more, something inevitably has to give. That something is education.

Do we any longer understand what education ought to involve and why it is important? On the one hand, we have the elders of the tribe, complaining that the National Curriculum is stuffed full of useless knowledge that must be swept away so that there is more time for the teaching 'skills' and 'competencies', celebrating the 'technology of teaching', and, ultimately, the demise of the teacher as lap tops are introduced into every classroom across the land. On the other, there are the politicians. Estelle Morris, for example, who wrote in the Introduction to last Autumn's White Paper, Schools Achieving Success, that 'to prosper in the 21st century global economy, Britain must transform the knowledge and skills of its population'. Education matters because the economy needs an educated work force. It is a brutally reductive, utilitarian view. We have forgotten that education, if it is anything, is a conversation between the generations in which the young are introduced to the best that has been thought and written by men and women who care about the subjects they teach – who care not because a qualification in their subject might lead to a better job, but because the subject itself is intrinsically important.

Sometimes over the last few years I have come to think that rational discussion is impossible. We have sunk too deep into a mire of accusation and counter-accusation. We watch the teacher union conferences on television every Easter and we see Socialist Worker Party members behaving in a way that most parents find totally unacceptable. The whole image of the teaching profession is tarnished. We listen to the Union leaders attacking the Government of the day for this or that and we despair at the predictability of their rhetoric. We ponder the slippery evasions of ministers who are as keen to proclaim their latest utopian initiative as they are to evade responsibility for the current crisis that is afflicting the system. It is easy to come to the conclusion that nothing is ever going to change.

Teachers blame the Government, the media and parents. Parents blame teachers and the Government. The media blames whoever it feels like blaming. The Government, if an election is not too imminent, blames the teachers. It is, it seems, hopeless. The vested interests are too strong, the egos of the individuals involved too big. Most important of all, standards, though the defenders of the public service faith will deny it, are too low. Is it hardly surprising that, according to a recent survey, over 50 per cent of parents would send their children to an independent school if they could afford the fees?

Or so at my depressed and defeatist worst I think. In more optimistic moments, I remember the hundreds of schools I have visited. I think of the many, many teachers and headteachers I admire, the thousands of very sensible and professional men and women doing their best to give their pupils a decent start in life. I remind myself of the gap between the twaddle peddled by politicians and the media pundits and the great and the good of the educational establishment and the down-to-earth common sense of so many of those who are actually doing the job.

I think, for example, of the teachers in a small and remote Cornish school that I visited two or three years ago. I had been invited down to open a new extension. The ceremonies over, I stayed for a while to have a cup of tea with the staff. I had driven from a meeting in London at which the literacy 'experts' had attacked the National Literacy Strategy. 'What do you think of it?' I asked my Cornish teachers. 'We think it is great', they replied. 'For years we have tried to ignore the different band-wagons as they have trundled past. Sometimes, they have come pretty close. But we have stuck to our guns. We get the results and we knew that our traditional methods worked. Now our approach has been vindicated'.

This book is for those teachers and their many like-minded colleagues. It is for parents and anyone outside the education tribe who from time to time has gazed in anthropological wonder at its curious antics. It is an attempt to understand what has gone wrong and why so that future governments can learn from the many and varied mistakes that have been made in recent years.

CHAPTER 1

Standards

I

The questions are obvious: How good are our schools? Are they good enough? Are they getting any better? The first, seemingly factual, shades inevitably into the provocative second. The third, which lurks dangerously beneath the surface of many educational discussions, hits the headlines every August when the statutory rise in examination standards is announced. The answers ought to be easy. We have the National Curriculum test data. We have the GCSE and A level examination results. Most schools have been inspected a couple of times by OFSTED. All we need to do is consider this evidence and, with regard to questions two and three, justify our conclusions. It ought not to be too problematic.

It ought not to be, but it is. Nothing in the world of education is straightforward. Everything, however cut and dried it might seem, is contested.

First, there is the adjective. Can we agree on what we mean by 'good'? Probably not if the discussion is between educationalists or politicians. Should children be taught to read at four or should we delay formal education, as some experts argue, until six or seven? Ought education in the new millennium to focus on the teaching of skills or does the transmission of factual knowledge remain important? Are school uniforms an anachronistic nonsense? The potential for disagreement is infinite. All too often, moreover, ideological disputes intrude into what ought to be strictly educational debates. The politician who froths at the mouth at the mention of grammar schools will defend his local comprehensive however appalling its exam results. A further problem is that many on the left bridle at the very thought of discriminating between and amongst schools. They argue that all such judgements are divisive and, because they demoralise the school that is found to be less effective, dangerous.

All is not, however, lost. In my experience, parents can and do agree. They may not think about it very much, but they want their children to learn to read and write. They know that progress through the system and, ultimately, a job depends upon qualifications so they take a keen interest in test and examination results. They know, too, that nobody learns anything in classrooms where children are running riot so they expect a good level of discipline. They want their children to be 'happy'. Which parent does not? They recognise that there is more to education than academic learning and hope that the school will encourage its pupils to be, for example, honest and responsible and loyal. They value sporting and cultural opportunities.

These are exactly the common-sense expectations that underpin the work OFSTED does in inspecting schools. In my view, they constitute, whatever the disagreements of the experts, a perfectly respectable basis for evaluating the performance of schools.

What, though, of the evidence? Can we rely on examination results and inspection reports to provide a definitive picture of the strengths and weaknesses of the nation's schools? I would like to be able to say that we could. I have after all been responsible for both the monitoring of the examination system and OFSTED. It would be a lot easier if I could simply confirm what ministers would like us all to believe, testify to the fact that everything is in apple pie order, and take a modicum of personal credit. It would be easier, but it would be dishonest. There are problems, particularly with examinations. We cannot rely on the evidence and until we can we will never have the schools our children deserve.

II

Let us take examinations first. A decent examination system will be sufficiently rigorous to sort out the good candidate from the mediocre; it will deliver results that reflect the candidate's unaided abilities; and it will be grounded in a curriculum that is worth teachers teaching and students learning. We do not have such a system. If our politicians were wiser and more courageous, they would admit to the fact and do something about it.

This is unlikely to happen under the current government. The U turn would be too dramatic. The many, Mr Blair has told us time and time again, must have access to what was once the province of the privileged few. All must have prizes. So every year the percentage of students achieving good grades in public examinations increases. Ten per cent of candidates achieved five or more good O level grades in 1955. The figure (GCSE grades A*–C) for 2001 was 49.8 per cent. From 1987–1994, the proportion of pupils achieving good results in 16+ examinations rose more than it had in the previous thirty years and by six times as much as it had the previous fifteen years. We will soon, it seems, reach that promised land where all do have prizes.

There are only four possible explanations for this apparently inexorable improvement in examination results. Each new cohort of students might be more intelligent than the last. Each might work harder. Their teachers might be teaching better. Or, as many suspect, the examinations might have become easier. The first two possibilities are fanciful. There is some truth in the third. But it is the fourth, which raises the terrifying prospect that we are living in an education cloud cuckoo land, that is the most likely.

The Government, the examination boards and the Qualifications and Curriculum Authority (QCA) that presides over them, the teacher unions and, of course, the students themselves do not want to know. They wouldn't, would they? The politicians want to enjoy their annual moment of vicarious glory as they gloat over the evidence that their policies are driving standards ever higher. Neither the examination boards nor the QCA is likely to admit that grade inflation has become endemic. The teacher unions enjoy thrusting the achievement of their members in the nation's generally ungrateful face. The students have (most of them, anyway) worked hard and deserve their moment of recognition. The creak of vested interests is audible across the land.

Back in 1996, the School Curriculum and Assessment Authority, QCA's predecessor, collaborated with OFSTED on an enquiry into examination standards. The result was a report entitled 'Standards in Public Examinations 1975–1995'. David Blunkett appeared to believe that this investigation came to the conclusion that there was not a case to answer. Estelle Morris and her officials take the same line. It is not true. The fact that, rather conveniently, the examination boards had destroyed the scripts from earlier years meant that we could not determine whether, grade for grade, students' work was as accomplished in 1995 as it had been in 1975. What we could and did do is consider how in terms of both syllabus content and procedures the examinations have changed.

Syllabuses, as you might expect, have changed very significantly. There is, for example, less emphasis on algebra in GCSE Mathematics than there was in the old O level. A-level English Literature students can now avoid studying major authors such as Chaucer and Milton. Less inorganic Chemistry has to be studied at A level than once was the case. The impact of such changes is, of course, a matter for professional and public debate. As one topic is dropped and another introduced, the examination may become more or less challenging. The point is that the debate has not happened. David Hargreaves used to argue when he was Chief Executive of the QCA that there is no point in looking back at all. The world has moved on. The examinations have changed. We cannot compare like with like. There is no point, therefore, in trying. Sorry, David, there is every point. It is the fact that the examinations are now different that is significant. It is the nature of the changes which have taken place that need to be brought out into the open. Ministers like Stephen Timms might then think twice before making their assertions that there is not a scrap of evidence to substantiate the accusation that the gold standard is in decline. The truth, I suspect, is that Mr Timms does not have the faintest idea what has happened to the examinations for which he is nominally responsible.

Neither, I imagine, does he appreciate the extent to which examinations have changed procedurally. Once upon a time, an examination was an examination. When I did my O and A levels and indeed my degree I sat in a room for two or three hours and did what I could to answer the question paper in front of me. Now most examinations have 30 or more per cent of the marks allocated to coursework. The argument is that traditional terminal

13

examinations test the ability to memorise and regurgitate facts while the clock ticks away. Coursework, it is said, allows the candidate to demonstrate the full range of his understanding and ability. In theory, it is an attractive idea. The problem is that nobody can be totally sure whether the coursework reflects the candidate's own ability. How much help has the teacher given? How heavily have parents been involved? Most worrying of all, has the student simply copied his essay from the Net?

Click onto the Elizabeth Hall Associates site and you will be offered 'anything you need written for your eyes only'. A range of such sites now exist to help GCSE, A level and degree students. One such, studyzones.com, marks students' work and suggests improvements that should be made before the work is submitted. Predictably enough, the examination boards are complacent. They have, George Turnbull, spokesman for the AQA board tells us, word scanning technology that allows examiners to detect repeated phrases. 'It is there, but we don't need it', he said. 'We are confident that we can detect cheating'. He is whistling, I fear, in the dark. A recent survey of 2,200 students in twenty-one American universities concluded that one in ten was using Internet sites to help them with their work. If we do not have a problem in England, then we very soon will. The legitimacy of examinations that rely on work done by the student in his or her own time has always been questionable. The new technology means that each year the question whether the work submitted has been produced unaided becomes harder and harder to answer.

The move to 'modularity' is a second, highly significant development. Nowadays many, if not most, GCSE and A-level syllabuses are divided up into modules, or units, of work. The candidate is tested on each module once it has been completed. Headteachers worry about the impact this has on teaching and learning and extra-curricular activities. Most feel that the intro-duction of the AS examination has reduced the sixth form to a treadmill that allows no time for anything other than preparation for the next wretched assessment. Many worry that a student who is unhappy with the grade he has achieved in a particular module can take the assessment again in the hope of achieving a better mark. Mr Timms needs to tell us whether he thinks this new facility has made public examinations more or less intellectually challenging than the traditional terminal examination. We could then have a proper debate.

It will never happen. The Government is determined to sweep any suggestion of grade inflation under the carpet. Look what happened last summer (2001). Angered and frustrated by the failure of successive Secretaries of State to do anything to stop the grade inflation he witnessed over the sixteen years he had been Principal Examiner in Mathematics for the Oxford, Cambridge and RSA Examinations Board (OCR), Jeffrey Robinson decided to blow the whistle and resign. The statistics he quoted are frightening. In 1950, 22 per cent of candidates passed the O-level Mathematics examination. That figure had risen in 1985, the year prior to the introduction of the GCSE examination, to 25 per cent. Since 1985 the percentage achieving a C grade (effectively a pass) has more than doubled to 55 per cent. Robinson does not subscribe to the better teachers/more intelligent students theory. His explanation is as prosaic as it is disturbing. More candidates achieve better grades because 'the marks required to pass at each of the seven grades (A to G) have been steadily lowered during the nineties'. In 1989, for example, the mark needed to obtain a grade C in the Intermediate level paper (the examination targeted at middle ability pupils) was 65 per cent. In 2000 it was 45 per cent. At Higher level (the examination sat by the most able pupils) the drop has been even more dramatic: from 48 per cent to 18 per cent.

You would have thought that the latter statistic would have brought a blush to the most brazen ministerial cheek. Eighteen per cent! We have reached a point where it is possible to get over four fifths of the questions wrong and still pass. In fact the Government's response was to rubbish the accusations and mouth the routine congratulations to hard-working students and their teachers. Doug MacAvoy chipped in for the unions: 'It is about time', he announced, 'the moaners and groaners accepted that examinations are not getting any easier'. And the QCA, the body responsible for the monitoring of examination standards, was wheeled out to reassure the great British public: 'We have every reason', a 'spokesman' intoned, 'to think improvements in grades are a consequence of hard work and better preparation of pupils and teachers'.

Do we indeed! QCA observers monitor the examiners' meetings where the decisions are taken to determine the number of marks required to obtain each grade. Never once in his sixteen years of examining, Jeffrey Robinson tells us, did any QCA official ever express the slightest concern. The royal 'we' might, it seems, be used to slide imperiously over a multitude of sins.

The only sensible conclusion is that we *are* living in cloud cuckoo land. The syllabuses upon which the examinations are based have changed, and, in the judgement of some experts, have become less demanding. We have coursework and modularity. We have the fact that lower marks are required to obtain each grade than was once the case. The problem is that nobody in authority is prepared to face up to these truths. Jeffrey Robinson's revelations prompted Ron McClone, the Chief Executive of OCR, to ask why we cannot celebrate the progress we have seen in examination results when we have no problem in accepting the fact that the four minute mile, which, in the early fifties, was the ambition of every world-class middle distance runner, is now the norm in serious athletics. The answer is, of course, obvious. In exam terms, the mile is no longer the mile. It is a few yards shorter than it once was and it is getting shorter all the time. If, moreover, we had seen the same progress in middle distance running that we have seen in examination results, the world record for the mile would be about two minutes. It is, in fact, three minutes forty-three seconds. In athletics if not examinations there is, it seems, still a way to go.

What, though, you might well be thinking, about the latest report on education from the Organisation for Economic Cooperation and Development (OECD) that was published last December? 'Worldwide tests put UK pupils close to top' trumpeted *The Times*. Estelle Morris was, naturally enough, delighted. 'Our children', she wrote in the *Mirror*, 'don't just match the best in the world – they lead them'. That, actually, is a bit of an exaggeration. We came fourth in the science league table, seventh in literacy, and eighth in mathematics. On the face of it, this was, nevertheless, good news, a genuine cause for celebration and, as the Secretary of State was quick to point out, 'a vindication of the reforms of the last few years'.

I hate to have to say it and I can only too easily predict the reactions of those who like to believe that I only want to criticize, but a few questions do have to be asked. For a start, it seems that the initial response rate for UK schools was only 62 per cent and that when replacement schools were added to the sample it rose to 82 per cent – which is below the 85 per cent the researchers deemed to be acceptable. Neither do we yet know whether this was a genuinely random sample or not. These doubts may be cleared up in 2002 when the delayed Technical Report will be published. There is, though, a more fundamental objection. Earlier international studies sought to cover core material from the curricula of the participating countries. The focus was simple: What knowledge have these pupils mastered? What skills have they learnt? This new study asks different questions: Are students well prepared to meet the challenges of the future? Are they able to analyse, reason and communicate their ideas effectively? Do they have the capacity to continue learning throughout life? Eminently sensible, you might think. Is it though? The whole project is 'based on a dynamic model of lifelong learning in which new knowledge and skills necessary for successful adaptation to a changing world are continuously acquired throughout life'. This is the fashionable twaddle I spend several thousand words dissecting in the next chapter of this book. What does 'dynamic' mean in this context? What, precisely, is this 'model'? We are never told. And the crucial question: how does it affect the definition of the different subjects the researchers are assessing? Mathematics is a good example – except in this brave new world we do not, apparently, talk about mathematics. It is 'mathematical literacy' now just as it is 'scientific literacy' and because, I suppose, they could not have 'literacy literacy', 'reading literacy', though the tests in fact assess the ability to write as well as read. Anyway, mathematical literacy is defined as 'the capacity to identify, understand and engage in mathematics, and to make well-founded judgements about the role that mathematics plays in an individual's current and future private life, occupational life, social life with peers and relatives, and life as a constructive, concerned and reflective citizen'. Fine, mathematics is more than numeracy, but the latter is rather important, and, while we may have come eighth in this latest international league table, the hard reality back home is that a quarter of eleven-year-olds have not mastered the basic competencies upon which mathematical understanding depends. What, moreover, is all this about 'life as a constructive, concerned and reflective citizen'? And, however sophisticated and imaginative the researchers, is it really possible to dream up a test that provides valid data about anything so nebulous? No, of course, it is not. We have, therefore, to approach this latest study with a good deal of scepticism. It is not quite the vindication Estelle Morris would like us to believe.

III

The other main source of information about what is happening in our schools is the inspection evidence gathered by OFSTED. Union leaders like Doug MacAvoy are as vitriolic in their criticism of OFSTED as they are determined to defend the integrity of the examination system. For obvious reasons. The latter churns out, year after year, results that always improve, evidence that can be used to defend teachers against the 'ill informed' attacks of the Institute of Directors and 'bilious' (the adjective is, I believe, the *Guardian*'s) commentators like myself. The OFSTED evidence raises some difficult issues and must, therefore, have been gathered by incompetent inspectors who, even if they were half sensible, do not have the time to do the job they are meant to be doing, and whose judgements are twisted to serve a right-wing political agenda. I discuss these misconceptions in Chapter 4 and want here simply to make the one point that is relevant to the debate about standards. This is that the Union allegation that inspection evidence is flawed because OFSTED is interested only in criticism does not stack up. Read any of the Annual Reports published in the years when I was Chief Inspector and you will see that there is plenty of praise. Indeed, looking back, the refrain is embarrassingly repetitive. My 1996–97 report opened with the sentence: 'The progress I described in my last report continued through 1996–1997'. In 1998 I wrote: 'The performance of teachers and pupils stands in sharp contrast to that of four years ago. Teachers are now teaching better and pupils, as a consequence, are learning more'. And in my last report, desperately trying to find new words to make the same point, I began: 'The steady improvements that I described in my last Annual Report have continued'.

Yes, of course, each of these reports contained criticisms. This is inevitable. Even Doug MacAvoy cannot believe that all is well with every school in the country. Neither, I imagine, does he think that the inspectorate should lie to the general public and Parliament. The Union opposition is to the principle of inspection, to the fact that schools are now accountable to the communities they serve. They cannot admit to this so they attack the integrity of inspectors, the methodology that underpins the inspection process and, above all, the impartiality of OFSTED as an organisation. More of all this later. The point here is that the unions have turned the truth on its head. If OFSTED has a fault, it is not that it has been too critical. It is that too often it has bent over backwards to be too kind.

A new headteacher has been appointed to a school six months before the inspection. She has clearly had an impact and the school is improving. At the time of the inspection, it is still, however, a failing school. What does the inspector do? Does he fail the school and (perhaps) demoralise the head and her staff? Or does he give her the benefit of the doubt in the expectation of further progress? It happens. How can the LEA that at the time of the inspection had the worst rate of improvement in Key Stage 2 test results in inner London be praised as a model of good practice? It was.

I am not calling the whole system of inspection into question. To repeat: I think that the weaknesses of the examination system are far greater than those of OFSTED. I am simply saying what ought to be obvious to anyone who reflects on the business of inspecting schools with a modicum of impartiality. The danger is that the judgements that are made are too lenient.

For two reasons. The first is that, contrary to union belief, inspectors are not driven by uncontrollable sadistic urges. They are human beings who do not find it easy to tell a headteacher who has invested fifteen years of his life in a school that he has made a complete mess of it. It is easier to fudge the issue and avoid the tears. The second is that, with the exception of the lay inspector who by law has to be included in every inspection team, every member of the team has extensive professional experience in education. They will have taught, may have run a school, might have worked as an adviser in an LEA or as a lecturer in a teacher training institution. The rationale is obvious. This experience is crucial if they are to have credibility with those they inspect and be able to make accurate and informed judgements about the quality of the teaching they observe. But so, too, are the dangers. They trail behind them the ball and chain of their professional experience. They drag the baggage of their beliefs about the nature of education, how teachers should teach and schools be managed, what it is reasonable to expect inner-city kids to achieve, into the classrooms they inspect. We all have our baggage, and, if we are honest, we know that it can be hard to jettison. Some OFSTED inspectors found it impossible.

If their baggage was the flotsam and jetsam of progressive education, then, in my judgement as Chief Inspector, we had a problem. I say 'in my judgement' because we are moving here into difficult territory. Parents might have their common-sense expectations, but the experts will, as I said earlier, have very different views on how teachers should teach and, indeed, on the nature and importance of the different subjects.

Take Geography. Do we think that our children need to know something about capes and bays and capital cities? Or should all this traditional stuff be dumped so that teachers can concentrate on the ethical dilemmas of conservation issues and exploit the subject's (I am told) unique potential as a vehicle for developing 'thinking skills'? What about History? Kings and queens and Nelson and Churchill? Or empathy and multi-culturalism? Should children be taught the alphabet and the sounds the different letters represent or is such explicit instruction likely to militate against their mastery of print and burgeoning love of literature? Each and every subject is beset by similar controversies and the world of education inclines, to put it mildly, to the progressive wing.

I can only say that my own stance, for reasons that I explain in Chapter 2, is unashamedly traditional. I wanted the inspectors who worked for OFSTED to approach the orthodoxies they found in some schools in a spirit of, at the very least, neutrality, or open-minded scepticism. Some could not. Some would not. Therefore, some of the judgements upon which my Annual Reports were based were, I believe, suspect.

Again, the significance of this admission needs to be kept in perspective. I shiver at the thought of the grilling I would have received at the hands of John Humphrys if I had had the courage to say this while I was still Chief Inspector. 'So, Mr Woodhead, it's all a complete waste of time, is it?' Or, alternatively: 'Ah [pause for dramatic effect] these stories are true then, are they? You bully all your inspectors into submission, do you? You tell them what to write and you won't publish anything that does not confirm your own prejudices'. Well, actually, John, no. I did not, it seems to me in retrospect, challenge them enough. I let too much be published in my name because I felt that I had to respect the professionalism of the individual inspector. It is a terribly difficult tightrope to walk this one, and I know that on a number of occasions I got it wrong. I fell off, even if, preoccupied as they were with my many other failings, nobody out there noticed.

I am not, to repeat, calling the whole inspection process into question. I am simply pointing to the fact, and it is a fact, that the judgements an inspector makes about the quality of a teacher's teaching will, to a greater or lesser extent, reflect his own ideas about teaching and education. My concern that some inspectors remained committed to the beliefs that in my view caused the problems in our schools is just that: a concern. It is not a fact. It is not quantifiable. It does, however, force me to say that the inspection evidence should not always be taken at face value. Like the examination statistics, it needs to be pondered, thought about, questioned. It needs to be read in just that spirit of open-minded scepticism in which, ideally, it was gathered.

IV

What, then, does an open-minded scrutiny of the examination and inspection data reveal? How well are our schools doing?

The current Chief Inspector of Schools, Mike Tomlinson's Commentary to OFSTED's 1999–2000 Annual Report makes a good starting point. He argues that:

> Improvements in teaching have gone hand in hand with rising standards in pupils' attainment at all levels of education, building on the clear gains made by four-year-olds. The proportion of eleven-year-old pupils reaching Level 4 and above in English has risen from 57 per cent in 1996 to 75 per cent in 2000, and that in mathematics from 54 per cent to 72 per cent. At General Certificate of Secondary Education (GCSE) level the proportion of pupils gaining five or more A* to C grades has risen from 41.2 per cent in 1995 to 47.4 per cent in 2000. Student performance at A level has also continued to improve: the average points score for each student taking two or more A-level subjects has risen from 15.9 in 1995 to 18.2 in 2000.

Teaching is now apparently unsatisfactory in 'only' about one in twenty lessons and the proportion of good or better teaching has risen from about 40 to 60 per cent. 'There is much, therefore', he concludes, 'to celebrate in our education system'. I agree, there is. I visited literally hundreds of schools when I was Chief Inspector, and, more often than not, I left deeply impressed by the commitment and professionalism of the teachers and the consequent achievements of the children.

That said, as we all know, and Tomlinson recognises, 'important problems remain'. He focuses upon the inability of boys to write a reasonably grammatical, decently punctuated piece of prose; deteriorating pupil behaviour; the failure of Afro-Caribbean, Pakistani and Bangladeshi pupils to achieve decent GCSE grades; the widening gap between successful and unsuccessful secondary schools; and the fact that the performance of a third of the LEAs inspected by OFSTED was found to be unsatisfactory.

It is a depressing list that will be all too familiar to anyone who has read earlier OFSTED reports and it prompts some very obvious questions. Just how much is there really to celebrate? How do we reconcile the optimism of Tomlinson's opening statement with this catalogue of problems? How much progress has been made in recent years? Is the Chief Inspector dancing to a 'be nice to teachers' ministerial tune? Is he doing his best to present the inspection findings as positively as he possibly can?

The answer to the last two questions is that he is. I did, too. He is perhaps trying a bit harder than I did, but essentially he is wrestling with the conundrum that became all too familiar to me. There has, particularly in primary schools, been progress. There is still, however, a long way to go and there are problems where we do not seem to be making any progress at all. What tone should the Chief Inspector strike? What is the truth?

Unhelpfully, the truth is that there are no truths. Or, to put it another way, one of the most significant and worrying facts about English education is the extent to which schools serving different communities achieve very different academic results. You may be lucky. Your children may go to a really good school. Equally, they may be stuck in a mediocre or failing school while you tear your hair out wondering whether you should remortgage the house to pay for a private education. It is a lottery. We do not have enough good schools, and those we do have, as so many parents know to their cost, are heavily over-subscribed. The best comprehensive schools have five or six times as many pupils achieving good GCSE grades as the worst. Some comprehensives have results rivalling those achieved in some grammar schools. Seven hundred, a quarter of the total, perform less well than the average for secondary modern schools. There are equally stark variations in the primary sector. Take virtually any LEA in the country. There will be very substantial differences between the results achieved in the best and the worst primary schools. At the age of seven, pupils at the top school are about two years seven months ahead in terms of their development in English, Mathematics and Science than pupils in the worst performing school. At eleven, the gap has widened yet further. In Mathematics the children in the top school are on average five years five months ahead of those in the bottom school. For English, the figure is three years seven months.

If we turn from the test and examination data to the inspection evidence on pupil behaviour, levels of attendance, and the quality of the personal and social education and pastoral care a school provides for its pupils, the picture is very different. Indeed, in primary schools at least, there seems precious little to worry about. The great majority of schools are doing an excellent job. 'Behaviour', we are told, 'is good in over eight in ten schools and unsatisfactory in only a very few. Pupils generally have good or very good attitudes to learning'. Incidents of racist name calling and aggression are 'rare' and are 'usually dealt with swiftly and appropriately'. Bullying is 'tackled quickly'. It is only, apparently, in a 'small minority of schools, often in areas of socio-economic disadvantage' that pupils' behaviour is a 'particular challenge' and even in these schools it is 'usually contained reasonably well'.

It is difficult to know what to make of these statements. If we accept what the unions tell us, they are wildly optimistic. Teachers, the unions report, are having to deal with more and more pupils who cannot or will not accept the conventions of normal schooling. We read not just of difficult teenagers, but of uncontrollable three-year-olds who have no language and no self-control, and who bite and scratch and spit. My own personal experience in visiting schools was that standards of behaviour varied significantly from school to school and, in less well managed schools, from teacher to teacher. I was also very conscious of the obvious fact that behaviour was likely to be better when I was around than it might normally have been. So, too, of course, during the inspection week. The inspection evidence may, indeed, be too optimistic.

In secondary schools, there are, as you would expect, more problems. Behaviour is judged to be good in three-quarters of schools, but in one in twelve (or nearly 400) schools it is unsatisfactory. Indeed, inspectors are finding more examples of poor behaviour than they once did. Why? Well, it might just be that, as many headteachers think, the Government's drive to reduce the number of children excluded from school has something to do with it. 'The available figures', Mike Tomlinson tells us, 'show that there has been a further decrease in the number of pupils permanently excluded from school'. He is too tactful to suggest that there may be a connection, but the very next sentence of his report reads: 'In too many lessons the bad behaviour or poor attitudes of a minority of pupils adversely affect the learning of others'.

Talk to any teacher and they will agree. I am certain that the strain of dealing with disruptive children is the single most significant cause of teacher stress and demoralisation. It is twenty-five years since I taught, but I can still remember my own feelings leaving a classroom where I knew that I had failed the majority of pupils because I had to devote ninety per cent of my time and energy to the two or three who sat in the back row determined to cause mayhem. Behaviour is an issue: for teachers and their pupils, for parents, and ultimately, for politicians. There are significant problems in many secondary schools, and though OFSTED inspection evidence suggests otherwise, in too many primary schools.

There are very real differences between schools when we consider other, less tangible aspects of school life. I have just been talking to a teacher who has moved to a new school. She went in a week before term started and was amazed to find that every other member of staff was too. In her previous school nobody had bothered to turn up until the day before the children arrived, and some did not bother then. You can walk down the corridor as pupils change lessons in some schools and have the door opened for you. In others you will be flattened against the wall.

'Of course', commentators who disapprove of parental choice will reply. It is all down to whether the school can attract enough bright, socially adjusted children from comfortable middle-class homes. There is certainly a vicious circle that can be extremely difficult to break. For whatever reason, examination results in a school begin to decline. The more concerned parents start talking. Some may remove their children. The school's reputation suffers. Its roll falls. It becomes a dumping ground for children who have been excluded from other schools. Examination results, not surprisingly, collapse further and its unpopularity deepens as staff leave to work in other, more successful schools.

But it does not have to be like this. An increasing number of inner-city schools are showing that the highest standards can be achieved in the most unpromising of social circumstances. If you walk down the Commercial Road in the East End of London and turn left after a few hundred yards, you will find Kobi Nazrul School. This is a school where most children arrive at age four unable to speak much, if any, English. 'So what?' is the teachers' admirably bullish response. The expectation is that these Bengali kids from appallingly disadvantaged homes have exactly the same potential as children who grow up in comfortable middle-class houses with the luxury of their own bedroom in which to do their homework. It works. By age seven, they can all read and many have exceeded the national expectation for English-speaking children. Last year's Key Stage 2 results were simply stunning. One hundred per cent of the children reached Level 4 in English, Mathematics and Science, putting the school amongst the top schools in the national league tables.

Kobi Nazrul is an exceptional school and as such does not provide a sensible basis for generalisation. Other inner-city schools are, however, achieving better and better results. We are still too dependent upon the charisma and dedication of a relatively small number of outstanding headteachers, but the bleakly deterministic assumption that high standards can only be achieved by leafy suburb schools becomes less tenable every year.

This is the good news about standards. It is not, sadly, the whole picture. We have, I believe, turned the corner in primary education. There is a light glimmering somewhere at the end of the tunnel, but it has to be said that it is pretty faint and that the roof could all too easily fall in as we stumble our way towards it. Too many inner-city schools are locked into a culture of under expectation and crisis management. Too many middle-class schools coast comfortably along, unaware that they could and should do much better. And if progress is being made in some primary schools, the sad fact, as Mike Tomlinson recognises, is that many children make very little progress when they move to secondary school. Some actually regress. Indeed, the more I reflect on the evidence he presents the more I wonder about the optimism of his opening remarks.

Let us turn for a moment to the more able students. Tomlinson's statistics suggest that over the last five years there have been significant improvements in results at both GCSE and A level. These figures need, as I have already argued, to be taken with a considerable pinch of salt. Suppose, though, we suspend our disbelief. Are they really that impressive? Recognising all the advantages that independent schools enjoy, let us compare the results achieved in the state and private sectors.

A glance at *The Times* analysis of last year's GCSE results shows that fee-paying schools occupied the top twenty places. 52.3 per cent of candidates from the 588 schools that belong to the Independent Schools Council achieved A* or A grades. The national average for all schools was 16.1 per cent. More than a fifth of the entries from these private schools achieved an A* grade compared with fewer than one in twenty in all UK schools. St Paul's Girls' School is, of course, even less typical than Kobi Nazrul, but it is worth just noting that a staggering 75.3 per cent of its candidates achieved an A* grade. The picture is the same at A level where forty-seven of the top fifty schools are private and the remaining three are grammar schools. Just one comprehensive appeared in the top one hundred. Five managed a place in the top five hundred.

I am not for one moment suggesting that it is sensible to make simplistic comparisons between the performance of a fiercely selective school like St Paul's and that of a typical comprehensive. Bernice McCabe, the headteacher at North London Collegiate, the selective girls' school that topped the A-level tables, said after her school's latest triumph, 'We have highly able girls here, excellent teachers, supportive parents and wonderful facilities. You would have to be actually bad at your job to fail'. She is playing down the importance of her own role, but she is right. These schools have huge advantages. That said, we would do well to resist the temptation to indulge in a quick fit of anti-elitist indignation. There are lessons to be learnt if we care to think for a moment about the facts that emerge from these league tables.

The first is that many of these top schools are single sex. We do not have that many single-sex schools in the state sector. Should we have more? The second is that, as we all know, they are selective. Are we convinced that a bright boy or girl in a comprehensive school is stretched in the way that their peers are in these independent, selective schools? The third is, yes, the classes are small and the facilities, as Bernice McCabe admits, often wonderful. But these truths should not disguise other considerations that might be as or even more important. The teachers in these schools are free to teach. They are not distracted from their core job by the bureaucratic burdens that afflict teachers in the state sector. They do not have to ponder the dubious merits of 'thinking skills' and waste time on the teaching of 'citizenship'. Their job is to teach the traditional academic subjects and the fact that they can concentrate on this core task must have something to do with their success. Their parents, moreover, pay, and, if we believe that the involvement and support of parents is important, as of course it is, then this might be significant. Should we contemplate the ultimate heresy and recognise that standards in state schools might rise if there were to be an element of parental contribution? And, finally, the failure of state schools to compete, explicable though it might be in terms of the advantages enjoyed by the private sector, ought to make all of us sit up and think. We can jump, of course, in one of two ways. For some the conclusion will be that we must raise tax until state schools receive as generous funding as independent, for others it will be a matter of acting upon some of the questions I have raised. What we cannot and should not do is ignore the size of the gap. To gaze upon the half empty glass might be depressing; to convince oneself that the half full glass is brimming over is to forget the distance that still has to be travelled and the radicalism of the action needed if that gap is ever to be narrowed.

This, however, is to move too far ahead in my argument. First we need to return to some of the other figures in the Chief Inspector's Commentary. He is, understandably, pleased that 'the proportion of eleven-year-old pupils reaching Level 4 and above in English has risen from 57 per cent in 1996 to 75 per cent in 2000 and that in Mathematics from 54 per cent to 72 per cent'. These are significant improvements. The achievement of Kobi Nazrul school raises, however, the obvious question. If a school in the East End of London serving one of the most deprived communities in Western Europe can teach every child to read, why cannot every other school? And most of the Kobi Nazrul children do not, remember, speak English as their first language. A target of 100 per cent is clearly a little optimistic. Some children, even at Kobi Nazrul in subsequent years, are not going to be able to make it. But it puts the progress made so far in perspective. There is no reason why the majority of children cannot learn to read. They can and they must.

Soon after I became Chief Inspector, I visited a secondary school in a pretty tough area of Birmingham. It was a good school. The head and his staff were absolutely committed and were doing, in my view, all the right things. Examination results were creeping up, but the progress was painfully slow. I asked the head how many of the eleven-year-olds coming into his school were able to read well enough to deal with the demands of the secondary school curriculum. He was embarrassed. 'It's pretty low', he said, adding quickly, 'My primary colleagues are, of course, doing all they can, but, well, you know how it is . . .' His voice trailed away. I understood his problem. He did not want to appear to be criticising his fellow headteachers. I nevertheless pushed him, and in the end, reluctantly, he told me. I cannot remember the exact figure, but it was well below 20 per cent.

I left that school deeply depressed. It was one of the experiences that led me to talk to Gillian Shephard, the then Secretary of State, about how we could not let things drift on, that we had to have a national literacy and, indeed, numeracy, strategy. It is the children who arrive in secondary school unable to read who give up, who play truant, who leave at sixteen with little or nothing in the way of formal qualifications to show for their eleven years at school. How would you feel if you had gone to school dreading the moment when you might be asked to read something to the rest of the class? If every day was one humiliation after another? It is appalling for the child and it places the teacher in an impossible position. We are still humiliating a quarter of our children. The Prime Minister would do well to remember this the next time he hears himself telling the nation that, having solved the problems of primary education, the Government is now turning its attention to the secondary sector.

The Government, of course, is in no position to solve the problems of either primary or secondary education. It can, if it so chooses, provide more funds for schools. It can threaten and cajole and encourage. It can launch new initiatives, or, if it is wise, it can refrain from launching new initiatives. But in the end it is the teacher in his or her classroom that matters. The better teachers teach, the more children will learn, and sadly, as logic dictates and experience proves, the converse is true, too.

Tomlinson's statement that 'only' one in twenty lessons observed by inspectors is thought to be unsatisfactory or poor is important. How do you respond to the adjective? I look back to the year before OFSTED was created and recall that inspectors were then routinely judging 20 to 30 per cent of the lessons they watched to be below par. We have obviously come a long way, and I said as much in each of the Annual Reports I published. Once again the statistic needs to be put into perspective, the exhilaration curbed. There are around 450,000 teachers in England. They teach perhaps five lessons a day. That is two and a quarter million lessons. One twentieth of 2.25 million is 112,500. There are thirty children in each of these lessons who are not making the progress they should. It is a lot of lessons and a lot of children. We cannot, as Tomlinson reminds us, afford to be too complacent.

There is another dimension to this. I do not know, but I suspect that the majority of these lessons are taught by a small number of incompetent teachers. If it is a good teacher who is having an off day, then there is no cause to worry. We all have our off days. If, however, your child or my child is being taught day in day out by a teacher who cannot explain things clearly, cannot inspire children to want to learn, cannot, perhaps, even keep the class in their seats, then there is a very real problem.

I do not kid myself. Einstein could have taught me and I would still not be much good at maths. Mathematics, however, is a sequential subject. If you fail to understand one concept, then you are going to find it very difficult to get a grip on the next. I spent a year in mathematics lessons learning nothing. No doubt I was partly to blame, but the teacher, who, shall we say, had trouble in imposing his authority on what was an admittedly difficult class, must bear some responsibility.

For as long as I can remember the problem of the incompetent teacher has been swept under the carpet. Nobody wanted the hassle. It was easier for headteachers and governors to shut their eyes and hope that whoever was complaining would give up and go away. The excuse has always been that it is impossible to sack a bad teacher. Time and time again, I have been told by headteachers that they would have done something if only the law allowed it.

The truth is that the law does allow it. Sacking a teacher is no more and no less difficult than sacking any other employee. The procedure, in principle, is straightforward: gather the evidence, explain the nature of the problem to the member of staff concerned, provide appropriate support, monitor progress, and, if there has not been significant improvement over a reasonable period of time, dismiss. It is not the law that stops headteachers doing what they know they should do. It is union opposition and the anger and hurt that can ripple through the whole staff. It takes courage, and in education, as in most other walks of life, courage is in short supply.

I first wrote about the problem of the incompetent teacher in an article published in the *Daily Mail* on the day that I became Chief Inspector. It was, I can admit in retrospect, naivety rather than courage that led me to say that teachers who were not up to the job should not be allowed to continue in the classroom. SACK THE INCOMPETENT TEACHERS screamed the headline. It was the *Mail* at its inimitable best. Gillian Shephard, who had just been appointed Secretary of State with, rumour had it, a brief to get the teaching profession back on side, was not best pleased.

I could (and still can) see things from her point of view. I can understand the argument that it might have been politic to be less provocative. I am nonetheless unrepentant. If I could turn the clock back, I would write the same article. No, that is not true. The piece I would write if I were starting again would be less coded. I would not leave it to the *Mail*'s subs to extract the real meat. The longer I did the job, the more convinced I became that shilly-shallying gets no one anywhere. Politicians and public figures seem to find it increasingly difficult to give a straight answer to the simplest question. The truth is wrapped up in cliché and jargon, buried in sentences so convoluted that no listener or reader has the faintest idea what is really meant. If Blair is to deliver his promise of radical public sector reform, he and his ministers must learn to speak plainly and honestly. It is no good saying one thing to one audience and the precise opposite to another. Radical reform means that people will be upset. That upset must be managed, but we will never make progress until our politicians have the courage of their pre-election convictions.

What, after all, is wrong with telling the truth? We all know that some teachers are incompetent. Most of us can remember one or two from our own schooldays. Those of us who have or had children at school will know how worrying it is to watch as your child's enthusiasm for school lessens by the day. Yes, of course, there are incompetent lawyers and policemen and, indeed, OFSTED inspectors. So what? The same rule should apply to anyone who is paid to do a job they cannot or will not do. We will never see standards rise in our schools until the profession faces up to this fact.

By 'profession' I mean, first and foremost, headteacher. If this sounds critical, it is. 'Seven in ten schools' might, according to OFSTED, be well led. That means, though OFSTED chooses not to do the arithmetic for us, that three out of ten are not. In one school in ten, leadership is 'weak'. One school in eight has made 'unsatisfactory progress' since its last inspection, 'often because of weak leadership'. There are 24,000 schools in England; 2,400, more if we focus on schools that fail to move forward, or even decline in standards from one inspection to the next, are poorly led. Yes, of course, we must congratulate those headteachers who are leading their schools 'well'. They are doing one of the most difficult jobs in the country and contributing more to our social and economic future than anyone else. Their success should not and must not dazzle us or prevent us from seeing that too many of their colleagues are failing.

I am not talking simply about the headteacher's willingness to confront the incompetent teacher. That is vital, but it is only one small part of the job. Secretaries of State and Chief Inspectors cannot raise standards. Headteachers can. Keith Joseph once said that the nearest thing we have in education to a magic wand is a good headteacher. He was right.

Anyone who has ever worked in a school knows this. Personally, I think back to my first teaching job at what was then Priory Boys' School in Shrewsbury. The headteacher who appointed me was nearing retirement. He was a rather remote, authoritarian figure who commanded respect, but failed, in my case at least, to inspire either affection or commitment. His successor could not have been more different. Warm, accessible, and energetic, Trevor Stratford went out of his way to encourage and never failed to praise when things went well. When they descended into disaster or farce, he could not have been more positive.

It was 1970, the winter of discontent. The big event in my year was the school play. Power cuts were threatened. Should we postpone until the spring when, hopefully, public order had been restored? Or, should we, having rehearsed ourselves silly and hired the lights and costumes, risk it? It was the biggest decision I had faced, and, possibly, in terms of the emotional turmoil, the biggest professional decision I have ever faced. We went ahead, and, sure enough, as Hamlet grappled with Laertes over Ophelia's grave, the lights went out and the funeral music ground to an anguished halt. The audience loved it, but I have to confess that it took me a day or two to see the funny side. It would have taken me a good deal longer if I had not had the great good fortune to have a headteacher like Trevor Stratford, who took the time and trouble to convince me over a pint or two in a Shrewsbury pub that a power cut, however personally traumatic, was not quite the end of the world.

Thirty years on, I have worked as an adviser or inspector with hundreds of headteachers. The good ones have spun their magic in, of course, very different and very personal ways, but they have all, like Trevor Stratford, cared deeply about their staff and pupils. They have had a very clear vision of where they want the school be in a few years time, and they have had their fingers very firmly on the pulse of what is happening in the classrooms and corridors of their schools.

The insecure head retreats into his office and shuffles bits of paper. He (and it usually is a he) is to be found more often than is good for the school he is meant to be running at educational conferences where he will stand up and read a carefully prepared question designed to demonstrate one or more of the following: the idiocy of government, the irresponsibility of parents, the inadequacy of his budget, the impossibility of the media, the criminal nastiness of inspection, and his own long-suffering, heroic stature. You can perm any option, but the latter is certain to appear. Good heads know that they are needed on site, that the most important thing they can do is be available.

It is a real pleasure to walk round a school with a good head-teacher. You are drawn into a hundred and one conversations, introduced to people, encouraged to share their enthusiasm for whatever it is that is going on. At the other end of the scale is the individual who is so full of their own self importance that if you ever escape from their office, which is unlikely, you never have a moment to engage with anyone. I was once taken round a school by a head who at the time had something of a national reputation. She did not acknowledge a single pupil, nor did she introduce me to anyone. I left with an empty heart, certain that the PR she had spun so effectively was just that. She has moved on now to a yet more prestigious appointment. With luck, the school might recover.

V

Are our schools good enough? The brutal, but honest answer is that they are not. If this provokes squeals of self-righteous union indignation, so be it. I know that there are many teachers and headteachers around the country who agree with me. It is their testament that matters. Individual teachers and schools are achieving outstanding results, often against appalling odds. Across the system as a whole, however, standards are too low.

Too many children fail to master the basic skills at primary school. Too many leave formal education with no qualifications to show for their eleven years of formal schooling. This is the 'long tail of underachievement' that politicians, educationalists and even union leaders recognise to be a problem. We are very good, the argument goes, at meeting the needs of the academic high fliers, but we have never really bothered about the less able. Is it true? No, on both counts. We invest billions of pounds in remedial education, trying, often unsuccessfully, to teach children who should have cracked the code at primary school how to read and write when it is too late. It is not that we do not care. We do. It is just that our response has been and still is so pitiful. The National Literacy Strategy might be a huge improvement on what happened before, but we still do not teach reading properly. We allow those who do not understand to fall further and further behind. And we wonder why we fail to secure, for all the additional resources and extra support, the progress we want.

Neither should we congratulate ourselves on the education we give to our brightest children. The Government itself now acknowledges this. 'In the past', states last autumn's White Paper, 'too many of our most able children have not done as well as they should, especially those from disadvantaged backgrounds'. It is tempting to point out that 'in the past' when grammar schools still existed in significant numbers, gifted children from disadvantaged backgrounds did have a route through to elite universities. If, of all newspapers, the *Observer* can recognise this ('indeed the proportion of state school children gaining places at our top universities has fallen since the dismantling of the grammar schools', 8 October 2000), then politicians might, you would have thought, have begun to examine their anti-egalitarian principles. This, however, seems to be a step too far. What we do have is the recognition that more does need to be done for the academically gifted. The problem is at long last acknowledged. The solution, however, is an archetypal New Labour bolt on. We are to have an Academy for Gifted and Talented Youth. 'Out of school opportunities' are to complement 'in school learning' – whatever this might mean in practice. There are to be 'world class' tests in mathematics and 'problem solving'. This is to tinker with the system. It is a tacit admission that schools as they are currently organised cannot meet the needs of the more able and that examinations are not sufficiently challenging. If Estelle Morris really wants to ensure that bright children fulfil their potential, she is going to have to face up to these facts. She must stop tinkering, and, as I argue in Chapter 7, undertake the fundamental reform that is the only way forward.

I am not holding my breath. On the evidence of the Government's summer orgy of congratulations when the examination statistics are published, there is little stomach for reality. Are our schools getting better? Are standards rising? Yes, if you believe the statistics and evidence. If, for the reasons I have already given, you approach this evidence with proper scepticism, you may conclude that there has been some progress but you are unlikely to share the ministerial jubilation.

CHAPTER 2

The Lunacy of Learnacy

I

Looking back, I am ashamed. I meant well, but too many of the children I taught as a young English teacher made too little progress. It was not, as some of my critics have alleged, that I was totally useless as a teacher. I had colleagues who were more expert in the craft of the classroom than I was or could ever have become, but I know that I was not one of my infamous fifteen thousand – the incompetents who should never have been allowed near a classroom. Most of the time there was reasonable order. A good deal of fun was had. My examination results were not too bad, so some children must have learnt something. A few might even have been inspired to love language and literature. I knew, though, that standards should have been higher. The penny ought to have dropped earlier. It should not have taken me the best part of ten years to understand that the problem was the progressive ideals that I had embraced so fervently.

I was too naive, too idealistic, and, above all, too gullible. I wanted to teach, but I did not want to be a teacher. I believed, that is, in the power of literature and the crucial importance of language. I wanted to help the next generation to appreciate the former and to learn how to use the latter. Note the verb 'help'. I did not see myself as a 'teacher'. When, as Chief Inspector, I read through the prospectuses of teacher training institutions, I used to groan at their refusal to use either the verb 'teach' or the noun 'teacher'. Their ingenuity was in a sense admirable. Students would learn how to become 'facilitators', 'mentors', 'learning coaches'. Whatever, the prohibition on the concept of teaching was absolute. Why? Because, thirty years on, the education establishment continues to believe the nonsense I espoused so enthusiastically as a young teacher, sorry, learning coach. To teach is to stand at the front and to bore the class rigid. It is to dictate notes and/or to expect the class to copy from the blackboard. It is to want your pupils to learn things that they did not previously know.

Teaching back in 1969 was a subversive activity. The idea that a school might be an institution dedicated to the pursuit of knowledge and the defeat of ignorance was passé. It still is. If anything, the situation is worse now than when I began teaching. Nobody believes that a teacher should be an authority in a particular subject whose job it is to instruct the young. Didactic teaching has no place in the new millennium. In article after sneering article, we are told that anyone who holds on to these traditional beliefs is a Gradgrind figure who has no concept of the power of the imagination, no understanding of how children learn, and no interest in the individual needs of the children he is teaching.

Gradgrind, you will remember, was a character in Dickens' novel *Hard Times*. 'A man of realities. A man of facts and calculations'. He looked down on his class and saw 'little pitchers before him, who were to be filled full of facts'. He was 'a kind of cannon loaded to the muzzle with facts' who was 'prepared to blow [his pupils] clean out of the regions of childhood at one discharge'. It is a terrifying testament to the forces of unreason that stalk the university departments of education and corridors of power in Whitehall that this hilarious caricature is now thought to be a realistic portrayal of all that was wrong with our schools in the bad old days before 'facilitators' and 'mentors' had been elevated to the centre of the education stage.

It was books like John Dixon's *Growth Through English*, John Holt's *How Children Fail*, and Frank Whitehead's *The Disappearing Dais* that influenced me as a student teacher. I remembered the boredom I had felt as a pupil listening to a teacher drone on and on, praying for the bell to end the interminable tedium, and I decided pretty quickly that, once I was in charge, my dais would be the first thing to go. It did, too. I could not wait to rearrange the pupils' desks so that they no longer sat in rows facing the front. I wanted them to work independently and to be able to engage easily in group discussion. The idea that they should sit gazing at me, hanging on to my every word, soaking up the wisdom, I and only I, could impart, was abhorrent.

I did not, you see, believe that there was any single wisdom. 'Constructivism' was the theory of the day. Children had to 'make their own meanings' and 'construct their own version of reality'. I did not want them to write down what I told them about *Lord of the Flies* or whatever. The factual information that I could transmit was irrelevant to the emotional engagement that had to be at the heart of every authentic literary encounter, and the more I told them what to think and feel the more inauthentic that encounter would become. My role was to help my pupils to feel their way into the text, to relate it to their own experiences and inner life, and to come, as independently as they could, to their own judgements and understandings.

As an ideal, this is fine. Teachers should not reduce poems and novels to comprehension exercises, and too often they did then and do now. Children should be encouraged to define their own personal response to the texts they read. The problem with constructivism is that it takes these obvious truths to a ludicrous extreme, rendering the teacher irrelevant and substituting the personal response of the pupil for the external authority of the text. In retrospect, I cannot understand why I found it so easy to forget that my own love of literature had been sparked in English lessons where teachers told me things about the author and the cultural context in which he wrote, pointed to interesting stylistic issues, and talked about their own reaction to the texts we were reading. English lessons where, in short, a good teacher taught. My own approach to teaching was forged in response to teachers who could not teach. I wanted to avoid the pitfall of their tedious didacticism, and, in so doing, fell into a different and probably deeper hole.

Most of us look back at our youthful enthusiasms and cringe, but I really do wonder how I could have been so silly as to subscribe to the ludicrous orthodoxies of the day. Did I actually believe that I would inhibit the child's creative flow if I corrected any punctuation or spelling mistakes? The answer is that I did, and I was not alone. The progressive line was clear. 'What message', the gurus demanded, 'do you want to communicate to your pupils? Do you want them to feel that you are genuinely interested in what they have to say? If so, the last thing that you should do is snipe from the margin and splatter their text with red ink as you rush to rub their noses in each and every mistake they have made. Can't you see how easy it is to demoralise someone who is struggling to become a writer?' Indeed I could. I can remember fuming with indignation at an anecdote in one of the seminal texts of the day about how a little boy wrote of his sadness following his mother's death. The teacher's response?

Isn't it about time you learnt how to use capital letters and full stops? Determined to demonstrate the depth and sincerity of my engagement, I would spend hours responding to my pupils' often very meagre efforts, sometimes composing a page or two of my own in response to half a dozen banal, misspelt, ungrammatical, scruffy lines. And, terrified of denting their blossoming authorial enthusiasm and fragile self-esteem, I would ponder long and hard before correcting a single mistake!

I was similarly nervous about grading pupils' work. I worried that a low grade would (you will appreciate that this is a recurring theme) destroy their confidence. This danger seemed, for reasons I cannot now recall, to be a more important consideration than the encouragement that a high grade, on the same argument, would bring. But my hostility to grading went deeper. I worried about what Ronald Dore called 'the diploma disease'. Students, Dore's argument went, ought to work hard because they loved learning. Intrinsic motivation was all. The grade in this admittedly somewhat unreal world was a potentially dangerous irrelevance. The last thing I wanted was to encourage an ignoble competition amongst my pupils to see who could achieve the best marks.

This line of thought led to an obsession with mixed ability teaching. A genuine comprehensive school would not, according to the purist orthodoxy of the day, contemplate 'setting' or 'streaming' its pupils according to ability. The damage to the (yes, you have guessed it) self-esteem of those unfortunate enough to be placed in the bottom sets would be irreparable, and, because they were in the bottom set, their teachers would never expect them to do well at anything. Excluded from the mainstream life of the school, they would sink further into failure as their more fortunate, intellectually able peers flourished in the high status environment of their top sets. How, moreover, could a streamed comprehensive school achieve its social ends?

In those halcyon, egalitarian days it was not, after all, the academic progress of the pupils that mattered. The real goal was social harmony: a good school was a school where the academic lions lay down with the remedial lambs; where the latter felt proud of their achievements, however minimal they might be; and where the poisonous divisions of class would be healed as children from different social backgrounds worked and played together. As I said, I was young and a tad gullible.

There was no Pauline conversion. Gradually, very gradually, my thinking changed. As a tutor in the Oxford Department of Educational Studies and, a few years later, an educational adviser working for a local education authority, I visited a wide range of schools. What I saw worried me. Watching other teachers struggle, I was forced, day after day, to reflect on my own failures as a teacher.

There were, inevitably, teachers who filled the lesson with the sound of dictation and expected their children to sit scribbling from the moment they entered the classroom until the bell, mercifully, signalled their release. Most teachers talked too much. Most still do, though whether it is an acquired habit or a personality defect I have never decided. Some fired questions at the class, keen, it seemed, to identify and humiliate those who had not yet understood. Such lessons, however, were rare. What was more usual and, therefore, more disturbing was the drudgery of classrooms where children ploughed mindlessly through worksheet after worksheet, where time was wasted in group discussions that within seconds degenerated into gossip and anecdote, where there was no urgency, no concentration, no buzz, and no progress.

Is it too harsh to say that such classrooms were the norm? Perhaps. But they were all too common. Why, I can remember asking myself as I drove home from one school visit in deepest Shropshire, is so much time squandered? Why are so many children so bored for so much of the time? Why are so many teachers so reluctant to teach?

Some, of course, were not and years later I can remember their lessons. A maths class, for example, in a primary school. The class was being taught as a class. The teacher was brilliant at asking the right child the right question at the right time. She orchestrated the lesson, drawing children into the work so that everyone was involved. She praised those who faltered their way towards a correct answer, but saw each mistake as an opportunity to help the class clarify their thinking and deepen their understanding. It was magic, and, talking to the children after the lesson, it was clear that they shared my enthusiasm. This was a startlingly gifted teacher, and they knew it.

So, too, at the other end of the age range, an A-level History lesson. The topic was the causes of the English Civil War. A lot of work had already been done. The teacher began the lesson with a resume of the theories advanced by different historians. It was a masterly blend of didactic exposition and questioning, that, as with the eight-year-olds in their maths lesson, engaged the interest of the whole class. One student argued passionately that the causes were fundamentally economic; another thought that political factors were more important. The teacher clearly knew much more than anyone else in the room, and his students knew this. He never, however, dominated the discussion. He would slide in a question that probed their thinking, insert a new fact or clarify a misconception. It was as far from Gradgrind as you could possibly be: a masterly demonstration of what teaching ought to be like, of how knowledge demands facts but involves understanding, and of how, if pupils are to learn, teachers must teach.

Did it really, you are thinking, take you ten years to reach this banal conclusion? Yes, I am ashamed to admit it. I was a slow learner. But, and it is a very big but, others were slower. I would not have felt the need to indulge in these embarrassing confessions if educationalists and the politicians they advise had now seen the light. They have not. Thirty years on, the same tired old, discredited ideas are exerting the same influence. If anything, as I said earlier, that influence has grown stronger. Academics, government advisers, media pundits – the great and the good who exert influence on politicians and public alike – tend to speak with one voice. I will give you some examples.

II

The Campaign for Learning is a 'national charity working to create an appetite for learning that will sustain individuals for their lives'. It seeks 'to make a reality of the Learning Age'. Malcolm Wicks, the Parliamentary Under Secretary for Lifelong Learning in the last Parliament is 'a great supporter'. So, too, is David Blunkett, who, when he was Secretary of State for Education wrote a Foreword to *Schools in the Learning Age*, a Campaign for Learning publication, in which he 'welcomed' this 'collection of essays from some of the UK's foremost thinkers and practitioners' and looked forward, he told us, to seeing 'how some of the ideas outlined in the book' could be 'applied in today's classrooms'.

The Campaign for Learning starts from the inauspicious assumption that 'these are more revolutionary than evolutionary times'. We are, apparently, 'on the edge of a paradigm shift which schools, like the language we use about them, are not currently set up to deal with'. Surprise, surprise, one contributor, Michelle Paule, believes that 'the sheer weight of content in the curriculum model inhibits learning by restricting the range of creativity of classroom experiences; leaving too many students engaged in accumulating information which they cannot see the use of beyond school, in order to pass tests and examinations'. Most of her fellow contributors to this book appear to agree with her. The challenge, she writes, is to discover 'a much more coherent approach to developing meta-cognitive processes'. She does not, I am afraid, give a wholly intelligible account of what such processes might involve. The editors do, however, make it clear that 'the task of the teacher' or 'learning manager' in the twenty-first century is to 'equip' young people with 'the basic skill of "learnacy" or learning to learn'. This, incidentally, is not a misprint. The word is 'learnacy', not lunacy, and the pedagogic implications are, helpfully, unpacked. Pupils will 'learn how to learn' if there is 'an explicit focus on the skill of learning to learn' so that they have 'structured opportunities to explore the cognitive processes involved in learning' and are helped 'to understand their particular blend of intelligence and learning styles and how they should develop these'.

Why, you might ask, did the supposedly sensible Mr Blunkett respond so warmly to this mishmash of tautology and gobbledegook? It is a question I could not begin to answer. It is perhaps significant that the man who was his key adviser, Michael Barber, is an enthusiastic advocate of something called 'multiple intelligences'. The term was coined by an American professor, Howard Gardner, who believes that 'all human beings are capable of at least seven different ways of knowing the world . . . seven human intelligences'. This is now an article of faith in University Departments of Education. So, too, is Gardner's conviction that because 'our educational system is heavily biased toward linguistic modes of instruction and assessment, and, to a somewhat lesser degree, toward logical-quantitative modes', children who have different 'learning styles' or 'intelligences' tend, quite unfairly, to do less well than those who are strong in language and logical-mathematical analysis.

The fact that there is no scientific reason to believe any of this worries nobody. Professor Barber, for one, buys the whole argument. 'So', he writes, 'the profile of intelligences is a starting point for changing approaches to teaching and learning'. He wants every teacher to understand that 'for any given aspect of the curriculum . . . there are at least five different ways to approach it and that these five approaches "map onto the multiple intelligences"'. Think about it for a moment. Seven intelligences, five different approaches, thirty children in the class. That is over a thousand permutations to hold in your head. Michael Barber, head of the Standards and Effectiveness Unit at the DFEE throughout Mr Blunkett's reign, thought that teachers across the land must assess all these different possibilities and decide, pupil by pupil, how they are going to approach every topic they teach. This is child-centred education gone mad, a pedagogic nightmare calculated to drive any teacher who has not yet expired under the weight of bureaucratic circulars to depart the profession forthwith.

Professor Tim Brighouse, Chief Education Officer from Birmingham LEA, was another of Secretary of State Blunkett's key advisers. Brighouse is famous for many things, not least his court action against John Patten, who, in the days when he was Secretary of State, was rash enough to question the good Professor's sanity. A more cautious soul, I will simply quote the first of Mr Brighouse's five predictions for the future as articulated in a *Times Educational Supplement* article:

In the light of research into the brain and theories of learning, teachers' questioning techniques will have moved (by 2050) beyond traditional methods. By then, we will be exploiting the alter ego dimension of teaching whereby they create an alternative persona to 'unlock the mind and open the shut chambers of the heart'. Evident first in the adventures of teddy bears and in the puppet theatres in infant and nursery schools, the technique is used by secondary drama, history and science teachers who make common cause in the use of masks and glove puppets to create alternative viewpoints.

I have not the faintest idea what Professor Brighouse is talking about. If my natural dwelling place is Tunbridge Wells, he inhabits an alternative universe.

David Hargreaves was until last December the Chief Executive of the Qualifications and Curriculum Authority, the body responsible for the maintenance of examination standards and the revision of the National Curriculum. Before that he was Professor of Education at Cambridge. He believes that 'all sixteen plus examinations must be abolished' so that the 'comprehensive curriculum can be . . . reconstructed or revised'. This, in his view, means 'a change of emphasis . . . from academic to social subjects and from the learning of information to the acquisition of skills'. John MacBeath has taken over from Hargreaves at Cambridge. Are his views any less predictable? No, I am afraid they are not. He dismisses out of hand the arguments of 'one Michael* Hirst who wrote that teaching was about transmitting essential knowledge from one generation to the next'. MacBeath knows better. 'We now know', he writes, 'that learning does not work like that . . . Far from thinking coming after knowledge, knowledge comes on the coat tails of thinking . . . therefore, instead of knowledge-centred schools we need thinking-centred schools'.

It is pathetic. Of course, the acquisition of knowledge involves thought. MacBeath confuses the pursuit of knowledge

---

*Actually it was Paul, but scholarship these days does not require an accurate recall of Christian names.

with the inculcation of fact. Worse, he seems to think that knowledge is an impediment to thought. The more ignorant the children, the more profound their insights. This, remember, is the Professor of Education at the University of Cambridge. What hope is there for state education when the academic who holds one of the two or three most prestigious posts in teacher education can write such twaddle?

The same meaningless dichotomy (knowledge v. thought, content v. understanding) underpins the thinking of Tom Bentley, yet another of David Blunkett's advisers. Bentley, like Michelle Paule and the Campaign for Learning, believes that the National Curriculum is 'too heavily defined by content at the expense of depth of understanding and breadth of application'. His solution? We must 'shift from a model of the curriculum based primarily on the formal specification of content, towards a more fluid but no less rigorous definition based on practice'. So that's all right then. The content has to go, but, don't worry, the rigour is to be retained. Quite how, he does not explain, though he does tell us that 'learning will be structured through projects'. A project is 'a piece of work, combining disparate resources, people and types of knowledge, to achieve a goal or concrete outcome'. Projects can, apparently, be 'individual' but many will be 'group based'. Thinking and self-assessment (buzz words in the moderniser's lexicon) will be 'embedded' (another favourite term) across the curriculum. Somehow Mr Bentley seems to think that along the way students will gain 'depth of understanding in a number of disciplines', including, he adds as an afterthought, 'traditional academic disciplines'. I can only say that I do not share his confidence.

The prestigious Royal Society of Arts (RSA), to quote their own blurb, 'is in a unique position to stimulate debate and to open the minds of government, education and all of society to the need for systemic change. Whilst other bodies discuss the curriculum, the RSA proposes to re-engineer education to focus on competences and embrace technology'. Should one applaud or quake? The latter, I fear, for this call to arms is predicated upon the belief that 'a radical re-appraisal of the aims and purposes of school education is essential', that 'current curriculum philosophy will be incapable of meeting the demands of the future', and that we need 'a transformation of the way learning is organised in schools'.

The author of the RSA report 'Opening Minds: Education for the 21st Century', Valerie Bayliss, states confidently that 'no one thinks education should look the same in twenty years time as it does now'. In one sense, I agree with her. Standards are too low. We do not have enough teachers. Too many of those we do have are demoralised by the blitz of initiatives and burden of paperwork. It is a mess. This, though, is not what Ms Bayliss means. She is convinced that the problem is 'a failure of strategy and purpose', a lingering commitment to a theory of education that will not meet future needs. Well, sorry, Valerie, there is at least one person who disagrees with you – me.

The quotation she parades from Gwyn Edwards, a lecturer at Goldsmiths College, fills me with despair:

> The basic assumption underpinning the National Curriculum is that the present and future needs of pupils, and the needs of the society in which they live, are best served by the study of an arbitrary collection of predominantly academic subjects. This highly questionable assumption should be at the forefront of any serious thinking concerning future developments of the school curriculum.

What is wrong with 'academic subjects'? Is Mr Edwards suggesting that English and Mathematics and History and Science should be abandoned? Would this serve the needs of either the individual pupils or society generally? His phrase 'arbitrary collection' suggests a rag-bag of odds and ends, any one of which could be dropped in favour of something else. Given that the school day is finite, there is always going to be debate about the inclusion of subjects that are not currently taught. Citizenship is one perhaps revealing example. But how many people really want Citizenship or Sociology or Astrology to be included at the expense of, say, History or Geography? Few, I suspect, outside the coterie of modernisers that are seeking to persuade the DfES, in the RSA's phrase, to 're-engineer education'.

Yet again, Gradgrind lurks in the shadows of the argument. 'The development of first an information and then a knowledge society challenges', Bayliss writes, 'a curriculum model centred on the transmission from teacher to pupil of a quantity of information'. Gradgrind filled his empty vessels, we, in our technologically advanced but educationally retarded twenty-first century, 'transmit'. Turn on, tune in, switch off. And it is 'information', of course, that fills the airwaves. Fact after un-related fact in classroom after classroom across the land. This for Bayliss is the reason why schools are failing to deliver. The problems we face in education, she writes, have 'little to do with the failings, real or assumed, of teachers'. They have nothing to do with the ill-judged interventions of politicians. The explanation, in her view, is our lingering commitment to an approach to education which values 'the acquisition of knowledge' and which reduces pupil learning to the mechanics of a crude input-output model: at best, I suppose she might say, an effective preparation for the quiz shows which dominate the real airwaves, at worst, as cruel and indefensible an activity as factory farming.

So, what does Ms Bayliss propose? What is the RSA curriculum for the twenty-first century? Well, it is nothing if not radical, for she quotes, apparently seriously, James Burke's belief that we must jettison our atavistic commitment to sequential thought:

> We all live on the great dynamic web of change . . . If knowledge is an artefact, and innovation is the result of interaction on the web, then the way for us to better manage change is to become acquainted with the interactive process . . . we might even consider changing our definition of intelligence. Instead of judging people by their ability to memorise, to think sequentially and to write good prose, we might measure intelligence by the ability to pinball around through knowledge and make imaginative patterns on the web.

It is 'competencies' that matter now, not knowledge, and it is upon competencies that the curriculum of the future must focus: Competencies for Learning, for Citizenship, for Relating to People, for Managing Situations, and for Managing Information.

Each of these broad headings contains a number of individual competencies. Students would be expected, for example, under Learning Competence, to:

- understand how to learn, taking account of their preferred learning styles, and understand the need to, and how to, manage their own learning through life
- have learned, systematically, to think
- have explored and reached an understanding of their own creative talents, and how to make best use of them
- have learned to enjoy and love learning for its own sake and as part of understanding themselves
- have achieved high standards in literacy and numeracy and spatial understanding

- have achieved high standards of competence in handling information and communication technology and understanding the underlying processes.

It is a revealing list. I am not sure about 'spatial understanding', but you clearly need to be literate and numerate if you are going to learn anything. ICT competence is also essential. So far, so good. I have, however, to confess that the remaining items baffle me. I am fifty-five years old and, though I say it myself, not totally thick. Have I 'explored and reached an understanding of my own creative talents'? Have I learned, 'to enjoy and love learning for its own sake', as part, mind you, of understanding myself? I have not the faintest idea what to say. For the last ten minutes I have looked out of the window at the Welsh rain trying to decide. My conclusion? The question is meaningless. I like reading poetry. Each poem I read, I learn, perhaps, a little more. Last winter I tried to learn Welsh. I found it very hard work. I am willing to try again, but I know now I am not going to 'love' the experience. Have I learnt 'systematically to think'? No, but I have learnt to think systematically *in some contexts*. Give me a political argument or an essay about a literary text and I can, for example, ponder the logic. I wince at the right places when I read a *Guardian* leader. Ask me to make sense of the instructions that accompany a self-assembly piece of furniture and my mind goes blank. Thinking depends on knowledge and confidence and it is context specific. The global objective is meaningless.

Do I, likewise, have any idea what 'my preferred learning styles' might be? Do I understand 'the need to manage my own learning throughout life'? No, of course, I do not. I simply do not know what Ms Bayliss is talking about, and I suspect that she does not either.

It may be me. But what about you? Do you 'understand

cultural and community diversity, in both national and global contexts'? Have you 'developed competence in managing personal and emotional relationships'? Do you 'understand what is meant by managing change' and have you 'developed a range of techniques for use in varying situations' (where, that is, I presume, change has to be managed)? Do you 'understand the importance both of celebrating success and managing disappointment, and ways of handling these'? Such feel-good ideas leave me cold. We might as well say that the school curriculum should produce the ideal human being. These aspirations are not 'competencies': they are what in this cliché-ridden age pass for counsels of perfection. Management jargon meets the gobbledegook of therapy and any possibility of education disappears out of the door.

The RSA consulted widely in preparing this report. 'A very strong view was expressed' in this consultation 'that the domination of traditional subject matter was so strong that no attempt to graft competence outcomes on to it could ever be successful; this would be true of both teaching and assessment. Only a complete break and the introduction of a new curriculum philosophy would secure the desired results'. God only knows what the desired results might be, but this is the threat we face.

I will end this Cook's Tour of current thinking about education with the 21st Century Learning Initiative and a paragraph that sums up many of our new millennium obsessions:

> The emerging multi-layered knowledge economy requires of all people far more than just basic skills. It requires creativity, flexibility, collaboration and the practical skills of the entrepreneur. These higher order skills are more effectively learned and developed in the rich, collaborative, problem-solving but uncertain world of apprentice type

learning than ever they can be in the formal classroom with its inevitable emphasis on abstract tasks and predictable results. Learning has to be about more than schooling.

Let us pause a moment. Gordon Brown and Tony Blair have told us that we live in a knowledge economy so often that nobody now asks what they mean, and, if the phrase means anything, whether it is true. Yes, our economy depends upon new ideas, but so, too, did every other economy throughout the whole of human history. Perhaps the point is that more people today have to be more knowledgeable than ever before? Sorry, 'the dirty little secret', to quote Robert Kuttner, 'is the scarcity of jobs that require more advanced skills'. The Centre for Economic Performance has calculated that 30 per cent of adults are overqualified for the job they do. As for 'multi-layered', I have not the faintest idea what John Abbott, the author of this wonderful paragraph, means. 'Creativity', 'flexibility' etc are, I agree, all important qualities. Three points do, however, need to be made. First, note the unexplained slide from 'knowledge' into 'skills'. Question: might not survival in the knowledge society demand just a little knowledge? Second, while 'basic skills' are, indeed, not enough, we must never forget that seven million adults do not have them. Until they do, we might well question the unreality of the drive to 'embed' all these higher order skills. And, third, the elevation of 'the uncertain world of apprentice-type learning' over the 'abstract tasks and predictable results of the formal classroom' is a transparent sleight of hand. Ask any teacher you know. Is it possible to predict what pupils are going to take from a lesson? Of course, it is not. This is true when we are trying to teach 2 + 2. If we are teaching, as I used to teach, a Shakespeare play, it is clearly ridiculous. 'Is Lear a man more sinned against than sinning?' Each student in my class would have a different view. None was predictable. The juxtaposition of 'formal/abstract' (bad) with 'apprentice type' practicality (good), is meaningless. Practical activities are essential to some learning; formal thinking and discussion and paper work equally essential for others.

'The primary purpose of education', according to John Abbott, the President of the 21st Century Learning Initiative, 'should be the development of transferable skills'. What is a 'transferable skill'? It is, Mr Abbott tells us, a skill 'which can be easily transferred'. As a definition, this takes the tautological biscuit. Can anyone, though, offer a better definition? Are skills 'transferable'? Does the ability to play the violin help you change a wheel on the hard shoulder? Does the ability to solve a chess problem help you to fix your leaking cistern? The answer is obvious. They are not. 'Transferability' is another of those much vaunted enthusiasms that do not stand up to a moment's thought.

Neither does John Abbott's next assertion. 'Now, at a time', he writes, 'when the half-life of new useful scientific knowledge is thought to be less than seven years, we are slowly coming to recognise that it is not so much what you know when you leave school that matters, as what you understand about how to go about solving novel problems'. Forget the irritating rhetorical flourish of 'half-life'. Suspend disbelief about whether scientific ideas do have a useful life of just seven years. Just pause for a moment to ask whether, even if this is true at the cutting edge of scientific discovery, it follows that children who are beginning to study science do not need to be taught some basic scientific knowledge.

You will not have to pause for long. Of course they do. The whole debate is absurd. You should not, however, underestimate the impact these ideas have already had on your child's education. The National Curriculum which, when it was introduced in 1988, was a challenge to both low expectations and the progressive, child-centred orthodoxies that had influenced too

59

many teachers for too long, is, for example, very much under threat. Its challenge has already been watered down as politicians have been persuaded to make the curriculum requirements more acceptable to progressive professional opinion. In English, for example, 'media and moving image texts' must now be taught alongside literature; history neglects chronological understanding in favour of 'historical interpretation and inquiry'; and in geography there is a new focus on global citizenship.

As Chief Executive of the National Curriculum Council (NCC), I was at the heart of the battle to ensure that the English Subject Order required teachers to introduce children to some classic texts from our literary heritage. Our efforts provoked 576 professors and lecturers in English to write a very indignant and superior letter to the *Times Higher Education Supplement*:

> As university teachers of English, we view with dismay the Government's proposed reforms to the teaching of English in schools. Like all academics, we expect sound grammar and spelling from our students; but the Government's doctrinaire preoccupation with these skills betrays a disastrously reductive, mechanistic understanding of English studies.
>
> Similarly, its evident hostility to regional and working-class forms of speech in the classroom betrays a prejudice which has little or no intellectual basis, and which is seriously harmful to the well-being and self-esteem of many children. We are all committed to the study of Shakespeare; but to make such study compulsory for 14-year-olds, as the minister intends, is to risk permanently alienating a large number of children from the pleasurable understanding of classical literary works.
>
> Even more disquieting is the plan for a dictatorially imposed canon of supposedly great works, in gross and

wilful ignorance of more than two decades of intellectual debate among literary academics over questions of literary value and the literary canon. These philistine, ill-informed proposals would strip English of much that we and many of our colleagues regard as most precious and educational about it. They threaten to reduce a living language to a dead one, and a vital literary heritage to a mummified relic. They would do serious damage to the moral and social development of our children, and to the cultural life of society as a whole, and all who are concerned with such matters should oppose in the strongest terms.

These academics might expect 'sound grammar and spelling', but they do not get it. They do not get it because for years grammar and spelling were not taught. This was no 'doctrinaire preoccupation', simply a pragmatic recognition that self-expression and creativity depend upon a mastery of the tools of language. Neither was there 'a hostility to regional and working-class forms of speech'. We merely wanted children to understand that different forms of speech are appropriate to different social situations. Why? Because too many working-class children do not do themselves justice in interviews. But it was the 'imposition' of the canon of 'supposedly great works' that caused most upset. 'Supposedly'? Dickens, Shakespeare, the Romantic poets? Do these professors really believe, to cite the infamous example, that Dylan is as great a poet as Keats? The answer, of course, is that, like the former Culture Secretary, Chris Smith, they do. I can only say that, nine years on, I remain unapologetic. The problem in English is not the 'philistinism' of those who believe in great literature, it is the relativism of academics who have spent the last two decades deconstructing the very idea of a canon.

The Geography and the History Subject Orders provide excellent examples of what has happened to the National Curriculum. Both subjects suffer from something of an identity crisis. The rationale for Geography tells us that the subject is important because it develops 'a range of investigative and problem solving skills' and 'prepares pupils for adult life and employment'. These claims are not, of course, unique to Geography. The argument that it is a focus for 'understanding and resolving issues about the environment and sustainable development' is a more subject specific, if ambitious, justification for its place in the curriculum. Yet more ambitious is the argument that it can 'inspire' pupils 'to think about their place in the world, their values, and their rights and responsibilities to other people and the environment'. Somewhere amongst all this there remains the fact that Geography is about teaching 'a knowledge of places' and an 'understanding of maps'.

At Key Stage 1 pupils are not expected to learn anything about any particular places. They are required simply to study the 'locality' of their school and somewhere 'either in the UK or overseas that has physical and/or human features that contrast with those in the locality of the school'. The specific places to be studied are left to the teacher's discretion, but must include a 'locality' in the UK and 'in a country that is less economically developed'. In addition, pupils must learn about three themes: 'water and its effect on landscapes and people' or coasts, 'how settlements differ and change', and 'an environmental issue'.

These 'localities' and 'themes' are the context in which pupils are to be taught geographical (e.g. field-work techniques) and general (e.g. how to 'collect, record and analyse evidence') skills. The prominence given to the latter is odd in that they are by no stretch of the imagination unique to Geography. The emphasis throughout is on teaching children to think about 'why places are like they are', how physical and human processes change the environment, and, in the section on sustainable development, how we can improve the environment. For better or worse, capes and bays have disappeared from view.

History has proved to be, perhaps predictably, one of the most controversial of the National Curriculum subjects. The argument has been between those who believe that children need to be taught about the past so that they have a firm chronological understanding of what happened when and those who are more interested in developing the skills of historical research and encouraging children, in the words of the Order, 'to see the diversity of human experience, and understand more about themselves as individuals and members of society'.

The answer, of course, is that both objectives are important. It has, however, to be said first that the phrase that I have just quoted above is awfully grand, and second, that too many of our children do leave school knowing next to nothing about the past.

At Key Stages 1 and 2 the Programme of Study is divided into five themes. The first, significantly perhaps, is Chronological Understanding: pupils should be taught 'to place events, people and changes into correct periods of time'. The second, Knowledge and Understanding of Events, People and Changes in the Past, follows logically if somewhat ambitiously: pupils are to be taught to recognise 'why people did things, why events happened, and what happened as a result. The next two focus on the 'process' skills which worry some people: Historical Interpretation (pupils should be taught to 'identify different ways in which the past is represented') and Historical Enquiry (pupils should be taught 'how to find out about the past from a range of sources of information').

No specific content is prescribed for Key Stage 1. In Key Stage 2 there has to be a local history study, a European study, a World study, and three British studies (choose from Romans, Anglo-Saxons and Vikings, Britain and the wider world in Tudor times and Victorian Britain or Britain since 1930). This is a list which clearly raises a number of questions: Is the balance between British and non-British history right? Will this approach give children any kind of historical understanding? Will it guarantee any kind of knowledge, however slight, of the great figures and events many people think should be part of our national understanding? These are rhetorical questions. If we really want our children to know anything about our history, then we need a different National Curriculum Order.

Not every subject has suffered to this extent and the National Literacy and Numeracy Strategies have certainly strengthened the English and Mathematics Orders. There is no doubt, however, that the pressure is on across the curriculum to dilute the knowledge requirements, and, indeed, to undermine the teaching of individual subjects.

Primary school teachers must now, for example, ponder the importance of 'personal, social, and health education and citizenship.' Mr Blunkett wanted the latter to become a formal subject in primary schools. As it is, teachers are expected to give their seven-year-olds the opportunity 'to find out about the main political and social institutions that affect their lives'. Children, for their part, must learn 'to understand and respect our common humanity, diversity and differences so that they can go on to form effective, fulfilling relationships that are an essential part of life and learning'.

Nobody questions the fine ideals. It is easier, however, to wax lyrical when you do not have to do it. We need to keep our feet firmly on the classroom floor, and, given the limited time available, we need to stick to the real priorities.

Should 'key skills' be a priority? There are six of them now in the National Curriculum. Three (Communication, Application of Number and Information Technology) are reasonable enough, but, in that they are already taught in other National Curriculum subjects, redundant. The other three (Working with Others, Improving their Own Learning and Performance and Problem Solving) are typical of the many woolly ideas this Government has embraced so willingly. 'All subjects', we are told, 'provide pupils with opportunities to respond to the challenge of problems'. In one sense, this is so obvious that it does not need to be said. In another, it is sinister because it elevates the solving of problems over the teaching of knowledge and because it is based on the false premise that the ability to solve problems exists independently of the contexts in which the problems are to be found.

And the accretions don't end there. We now have 'thinking skills' in the National Curriculum. We have 'financial capability'. We have 'enterprise education'. We have 'education for sustainable development'. And, as an inevitable consequence, we have less and less time for the teaching of the subjects the National Curriculum was first introduced to protect. What do we want our children to learn at school?

III

No question in the drive to raise standards is more important. 'It is ideas', the economist John Maynard Keynes wrote in 1936, 'which are dangerous for good or evil'. Ideas, he argued, are more dangerous even than vested interests. He was right. If the ideas that determine what a teacher does in his classroom are woolly, simplistic or otherwise corrupt, then our children will suffer, and it is the children who have no books at home who will suffer the most. The tragedy is that Ms Morris and her officials do not seem to understand this basic truth. They tinker endlessly with structures, they pour millions of pounds into one wrong-headed initiative after another, and, in the middle of the night they must, once in a while, wonder why on earth standards are not rising. The answer is obvious. Pursue the wrong educational goals and the reform programme will grind deeper and deeper into the sand. That is what is happening. The battle of ideas is crucial. It must be won.

CHAPTER 3

Teachers and Teaching

I

To return to the most obvious and basic truth of all: what matters most is the professionalism of the individual teacher. The more effective the teacher, the greater the progress the pupil will make. Of course, but what do we mean by 'professionalism' and what can we do to ensure that we have the quantity and quality of teachers we need if our children are to receive the education they deserve?

When the teacher unions accuse the Government of 'de-professionalising' teachers, as they so often do, they mean that Parliament has had the temerity to pass laws they do not like. They did not like the National Curriculum. They did not like the National Literacy and Numeracy Strategies. They hated the idea of performance pay. The National Curriculum was bad because it told teachers what they had to teach. The trade union argument is that teachers should have complete freedom to teach their pupils whatever they want. Indeed, they clearly think that it is only the teacher in his classroom who, knowing his subject and his children, has the professional competence to come to a sensible decision about what subject matter is appropriate and what is not. The National Literacy and Numeracy Strategies were condemned because they, too, intruded into what, it was felt, ought to be an unassailable professional domain. They were worse, even, than the National Curriculum, for they went beyond the specification of content to define how a teacher should teach. This was the ultimate arrogance on the part of the politicians and the final humiliation for teachers. And performance pay was bad, well, because it was 'elitist' and 'divisive' and the unions in their collective, professional wisdom did not want it.

You may feel that the unions were right in each of these cases to complain, but this is not the point. What is significant here is the assumption that the professional, because he knows (or thinks he knows) what is best, has the right (indeed, some would argue, the responsibility) to resist decisions taken by a democratically elected government. The unions do not appear to think that there is an alternative and legitimate point of view. I do. Like David Marsland, the Director of the Centre for Evaluation Research at Brunel University, I believe that 'teachers have no right at all qua teachers and in their professional role to resist, and certainly not to sabotage, particular forms of school organisation or curricular patterns or assessment procedures if they have been determined by due process by an elected government. As citizens, of course, we can campaign as we wish – but not as teachers as such. As professionals we should do no more than present the evidence persuasively, and, if we lose the argument, buckle down'.

Buckle down, the unions have not. They have done their best to prevent virtually every reform this government and the last Conservative Government have sought to introduce. On some occasions they have won. Performance pay is a good example.

The Prime Minister wanted a system that rewarded and motivated good teachers. The unions did not. We have ended up with a situation in which virtually every teacher who applied to go through the so-called 'threshold' has received an extra £2,000. This cannot, by any stretch of the imagination, be a genuine system of performance pay. Once through the threshold, always through the threshold. There is no annual assessment of performance against objectives and, therefore, no question of any pressure or elitist division into the successful sheep and incompetent goats. Game, set and match, in fact, to the unions. When, moreover, the unions fail to prevent legislation, they simply continue to resist. Their threats, for example, of industrial action in 1993 over the National Curriculum forced the Government into a radical revision of the National Curriculum as it then was. The fact that the National Curriculum may have needed some reform is neither here nor there. The issue is, first, whether teachers can reasonably demand an autonomy so complete that they can ignore or subvert the law, and, second, the impact union intransigence of this kind has on the public perception of teachers.

Marsland is very clear. Full autonomy, he argues, is available only to independent practitioners. Teachers cannot reasonably expect on the one hand to enjoy the job security they have as state employees, and, on the other, to ignore the legitimate instructions of their political masters. He goes on to argue that the public has come to see teachers 'as political rather than professional agents' and that 'a significant degree of the public trust upon which the establishment and maintenance of professional autonomy depends has been lost'. The moral is obvious. If teachers want to be treated as professionals, they must start to act professionally.

This means, of course, that they must deliver the results parents expect. The better teachers teach, the more children learn.

The more children learn, the higher their reputation in the communities they serve. The higher that reputation, the more likely it is that, as trusted professionals, they will be left to manage their own affairs. Public esteem has to be earned. If the public has a low opinion of teachers, it is, in part at least, because too many teachers have for too long failed to teach their children. This is, or ought to be, obvious. It is not to Messrs MacAvoy, De Gruchy and Smith, the general secretaries of the three main teacher unions. They have no concept of professionalism, only of deprofessionalisation. Anyone and everyone is responsible for the low standing of teachers. Politicians, parents, the media, me – but not, of course, teachers and certainly not the unions that are meant to represent their interests.

This statement by the eloquent and incisive John Bangs, Head of Education at the NUT, is, for example, typical of the union line:

Teachers are very demoralised by being undermined all the time on their practices. For mature teachers that's a terrible thing to say. They ought to be leading and being mentors and helping young teachers. The challenge is how you get back a profession that believes fundamentally in constantly renewing itself in terms of learning, that means having professional development integral to what you do, teachers as researchers – there's a great disdain among the academic establishment of the idea that teachers can be researchers – having teachers feeling that the hours they are doing are worth it and they are in control of the number of hours they are doing. Schools have got to be far more than delivery agents, they've got to be schools as communities. The issue now is how to embed the fundamental reforms – the literacy and numeracy strategies – so that teachers own them. Because if you don't, they will just fall back, all that investment will be for nothing. The main problem is how you actually build the morale and professional confidence of teachers to take all the issues in the profession and say: 'Well, actually, we trust you'.

It is depressing, isn't it? Who or what is this mysterious 'you' that is meant to raise morale? I have no idea, and I am pretty sure that Mr Bangs does not know either. What is clear is the abnegation of professional responsibility. If morale is low, it is 'our' fault because we do not trust teachers enough. The fact that trust, in teaching as in any other area of human activity, has to be earned seems to have escaped Mr Bangs' blinkered, self-righteous consciousness. The ball, John, is in the profession's court. Run with it and morale will rise. Sink supine and resentful and you make matters worse. It is obvious to everyone other than the diehard union activists.

Interestingly, many teachers know that their union spokesmen do them no favours. They question the totally predictable defence of the status quo. How, they ask, can organisations which purport to represent professionals do everything in their power to protect mediocre and incompetent teachers who have brought the profession into disrepute? Why should a teacher's remuneration not be in part determined by his performance in the classroom? What is wrong with competition between schools? Is it reasonable to argue that all schools, irrespective of their success and popularity, should be allocated the same 'fair' share of students and resources? Is it really sensible to oppose any move to contract out education functions from the public to the private sectors as a matter of ideological faith?

The stock union response is that what is good for teachers is good for children. Oh yes? Talk to any headteacher across the country and they will tell you that it is difficult to sack an incompetent teacher. Why? In part, because, despite their public protestations to the contrary, the unions will resist tooth and nail. Is this really in the pupils' interests? Of course it is not. How can organisations that want us to believe that they are as committed to the drive to raise standards as any politician in the run up to an election oppose the evaluation of a teacher's performance on the basis of what his children learn? They cannot. The self interest is transparent and the damage done over the years to the reputation of teachers huge.

The Government believes that 'the creation of the General Teaching Council (GTC) marks an important step in strengthening teachers' professional status'. It is a step, if anything, in the wrong direction: a sixty-four strong talking shop, with nine union representatives and thirteen Secretary of State appointees that is chaired by a former film producer. It has done nothing memorable in the first year of its existence, other than to rehearse, predictably enough, the usual prejudices and platitudes. Go, for example, to its web site (which is notable for the absence of any specific GTC policy proposals) and you will find some University of North London research on why teachers are leaving the profession. The most common cause, according to this research, is that teachers want 'more professional autonomy and more opportunities for creativity and working with adults'. Should one laugh or cry? You know, surely, if you chose teaching as a career, that it is a job that involves spending the odd hour or two working with children? In my naivety, I thought that is why teachers chose to teach. Note the way in which the tired old clichés about 'autonomy' and 'creativity' are trotted out without any thought or analysis. The GTC line is identical to that of the unions. The National Curriculum and the National Literacy and Numeracy Strategies have driven the fun and professionalism out of teaching.

Morale will be restored if teachers are more involved, whatever in practice this might mean, in the formulation of new policy initiatives.

The GTC is not going to deliver. Professor Marsland is probably right. What is needed is 'an authentic grass roots movement among teachers rather like a religious revival which – entirely regardless of resources, or administrative structures or salaries, or official training standards – strives for the establishment of real professionalism'. More headteachers and teachers need to put their heads above the parapet and 'criticise and publicly condemn inadequates among recruits to teaching, hopeless training courses and colleagues (including headteachers and inspectors) whose primary goals are political rather than educational'. Will it happen?

Fanciful though it sounds, it might. Teachers are frustrated and depressed. They do not feel that their professionalism, by which I mean their classroom expertise and idealistic concern for the children they teach, is properly recognised. Many have little time for the knee-jerk negativity and high-falutin' rhetoric of their unions. They resent a government that treats what ought to be a profession as if it were a class of five-year-olds in need of constant reassurance and the occasional Smartie. What alternative is there? The time might just be ripe.

II

There is, however, a further problem. The Government believes that the teaching profession, along with local education authorities, the funding system, school buildings and pretty well everything else, must be 'modernised'. If this were to mean the introduction, for example, of a genuine system of performance pay that rewarded outstanding teachers or some serious thought about how the more intelligent use of administrative staff and classroom assistants could allow teachers to focus on their core teaching responsibilities, then I would applaud. I suspect, however, that rather more is intended, and that, once again, teachers are likely to be distracted from the pursuit of better subject knowledge and stronger practical pedagogical skills upon which their professionalism depends.

The guru here is Professor David Hargreaves, who resigned last year as Chief Executive of the Qualifications and Curriculum Authority and is now a Special Adviser to Estelle Morris. Hargreaves believes that 'teachers and schools must stop serving as role models for fading career structures and moribund communities and begin to model people who are team playing, networking and community supporting, with an ability to be continually creative in a world in which, by definition, fresh problems unfold but must be solved quickly and creatively'. So, there you go. Are you up for it? Can you team play, network and community support your way into this continuously creative future? Or, shame on you, are you locked into your fading career and moribund community? The good Professor continues. Teaching, he tells us, 'must become a profession in which able graduates believe they can play innovative roles in the task of professional and institutional re-shaping that is required with the emergence of the knowledge society'. Read quickly, such sentences can impress as heady, inspirational stuff; skimmed, they might, for a moment or two, even appear to mean something. What is this 'knowledge society'? Why, if it exists, does Hargreaves assume that schools must respond to it and assume a radical new identity? What, exactly, is the task of professional and institutional re-shaping?

And so on. Meaningless or not, this is the level of rhetoric able graduates encounter. It is the rhetoric that makes, I suspect, a good number decide that teaching is the last thing they want to do. Neither is it just a matter of individual academics like David Hargreaves. A gullible government that likes nothing better than a sentence or two of cutting edge, modernising guff has convinced itself that the future depends on our ability to 'transform' the teaching profession and develop what Hargreaves calls 'knowledge creating schools'.

The argument is that the education service has to develop 'new professional knowledge'. Fine, but what is it? I do not know. Neither does Hargreaves. Nowhere in his sixty-page pamphlet *Creative Professionalism* is there an actual example. He writes, at considerable length, about the process of knowledge creation. He cites some underwhelming 'testimony' from teachers who have the good fortune to work in 'knowledge creating schools' (a teacher who, for example, espouses 'the virtues of thinking skills', a headteacher who seems rather pleased that he 'spends quite a bit of time out of school, talking with our partners and keeping an eye open for any new ideas or opportunities'). Nowhere does he tell us what these new pedagogic and managerial understandings might involve. Nobody ever does. Nobody ever does because nobody ever can. They do not exist.

Nonetheless, the chase continues and the real understandings teachers need recede further and further into the distance. Think back to your own childhood and reflect for a moment on the teachers who influenced you. What did they have in common? Four things in my experience. They were men and women who cared about their pupils as individuals. They wanted and expected you to learn. They were enthusiastic about their subject and, last but not least, they knew how to teach. None of this is very surprising and that, of course, is the point. 'When you start talking about teaching', as Jonathan Smith, who taught for thirty years at Tonbridge, wrote recently, 'it is difficult not to sound as if you are stating the obvious.

Because . . . well, you are'. Perhaps this is why the gurus are driven to ever more fanciful and obscurantist accounts of how teaching in the twenty-first century must be transformed from its boring old nineteenth- and twentieth-century self. But, as Smith adds, 'it is obviousness of a tricky kind'. I am not for one moment suggesting it is easy. Neither do I hark back to some pre-lapsarian pedagogic Utopia. Some ages were more golden than others, but none was so golden that it provides a model for the future. The challenge is to identify and hold on to the essential truths about teaching, the traditional wisdom that worked then, works now, and will work equally well in future millennia.

The greatest challenge seems, if you are a Professor of Education, to be to keep your feet on the classroom floor. Take the first and most basic truth of all. 'You have to keep order', as Miss Harby reminds Ursula in D. H. Lawrence's *The Rainbow*, 'if you want to teach'. Indeed you do. 'Children will never naturally acquiesce to sitting in a class and submitting to knowledge. They must be compelled to by a stronger, wiser will. Against which they must always strive to revolt'. That is Lawrence again, who taught for three years at Davidson Road School in Croydon, and who never forgot. If they ever knew, the great and the good who pontificate about the twenty-first century teacher invariably do. Here is John MacBeath, Professor of Education at Cambridge University, waxing lyrical about 'the post-millennium classroom':

A good starting place for intellectual subversion is to encourage pupils to ask the question: 'Why are you teaching this to me today?'. We have found time and time again in our research that, when pupils and teachers together explore learning, some of the most deeply ingrained beliefs and prejudices are opened to question . . .

76

Sorry, Mr MacBeath. It is your 'prejudices' that need to be questioned, and God knows where you did it, your research that must be challenged. In my experience as a pupil, a teacher and an inspector, 'intellectual subversion' is not a behaviour that needs to be encouraged. Yes, I know. *The Rainbow* was written in 1916. Poor Ursula, Lawrence's idealistic young teacher, had forty-five children in her class. So what? 1916 or 2016, fifty-five or twenty-five, it does not matter. The will of the teacher must be imposed on the will of the children.

The second truth is that teachers and children do not 'learn together'. It is the children who learn. The teacher teaches. Two simple little sentences and I have sat here for half an hour wondering whether I have the courage to let them stand. Why? Because they challenge head-on the collective wisdom that dominates current thinking about the nature of education and the job of the teacher. I can envisage the protest only too well. So be it. The teacher ought to teach. To quote Jonathan Smith again: 'the best teachers, in my experience, tell you things. Now the pupil is told less, and yet, paradoxically, the less he is told the more he is being told to think for himself'. That, in a nutshell, is the absurdity of today's orthodoxy. And the Union general secretaries wonder why the public do not have a high opinion of the teaching profession!

What does the Secretary of State, Estelle Morris, think? Does she understand the problem? Does she intend to implement a programme of reform that will challenge the orthodoxy and enhance teacher professionalism?

She does not, in my view, understand and I do not think that the initiatives she is pursuing will ever deliver the improvements we need. Indeed, penetrate the verbiage ('the challenge of radical modernisation in our comprehensive schools is the challenge of meeting the needs of each and every child') and read between the lines of last autumn's White Paper and the depth of her incomprehension is all too clear. She tells us, for example, that the Government's strategy to raise standards at the bottom end of the secondary school is designed to 'offer support to all teachers of all subjects to improve their skills in providing feedback to pupils on their work, setting individual targets for pupils and teaching reasoning and logical and creative thinking through their subject'. She applauds the fact that the 'new technology can enable teachers to tailor their teaching more closely to the abilities of individual pupils'. A 'Schools' Innovation Unit' is to be established 'to encourage and respond to innovative approaches to teaching and learning'. Predictably, the precise nature of these innovative approaches is left vague, but the general drift is clear. Teachers must focus on the individual needs of pupils, 'thinking skills' are more important than subject knowledge, the name of the game is innovation.

It sounds fine, doesn't it? What, for example, is wrong with trying to find ways to tailor teaching to the needs of individual pupils? The answer is everything. The best teachers, remember, tell you things. How can any teacher, however gifted, however sophisticated he may be in using new technology, tell thirty pupils thirty different things? If the lesson is one hour long, he has two minutes maximum with each pupil. And while he is working with the one pupil, what are the remaining twenty-nine doing? Working perhaps. But, then again, perhaps not. Whatever they are doing, they are not benefiting from the teacher's knowledge. They are not being told anything.

Do not, moreover, assume that all would be well in a smaller class. The Government wants us to applaud the fact that it has reduced class sizes by a pupil or two in Key Stage 1. We should sit on our hands. It is not that we now have bigger classes higher up the school. It is not even that tiny reductions of this order make no difference at all. Neither would far larger reductions. This is the fundamental point. Suppose, though no government could ever afford to do it, our theoretical class of thirty is reduced by 50 per cent. Fifteen pupils, one teacher, a lesson that lasts an hour. The arithmetic is not that difficult. Each pupil now has the princely total of four minutes of the teacher's attention. The fact that the size of the class has been halved makes, in practice, little difference. The belief that teachers must cater for individual needs (let alone adapt their pedagogy to a pupil's favoured 'learning style' or 'dominant intelligence') is a dangerous nonsense. We must return to the traditional idea of the teacher teaching the class. This is truth three.

Truths four and five follow. Truth four is that whole class teaching is only possible when pupils have a firm grip on the concepts needed to make sense of whatever it is that is being taught. If they do understand, the size of the class is an issue, but it is not the key issue. More children will be able to participate in a class of fifteen than a class of thirty. However, the key factor that determines the quality of learning is the quality of teaching. Which would you want for your child? A class of fifteen that spends its time fooling around because the teacher cannot keep control, or a class of thirty where every moment is spent, in the jargon, 'on task' because the teacher knows how to teach? If some pupils do not understand, then, again, the number in the class is largely an irrelevance, for no teacher, however brilliant, can help the child who is struggling to grasp the basic concept when other children want far more demanding instruction. The key practical question, therefore, is this: how can schools ensure that pupils in a class are in a position to understand the new knowledge that is being taught?

Small schools cannot. They have to do the best they can. Some, because of the dedication and skill of their teachers, do very well. They would do better if they could group their pupils in terms of their ability in different subjects. In larger schools it is possible, but only if three conditions are met. The first is that the sequence of teaching and learning, the hierarchy of concepts that have to be mastered, is very carefully defined in each subject. The second is that mastery of each concept is tested before the pupil moves to the next stage in the subject. The third is that the school is able to offer extra teaching to the pupils who do not understand first time round.

Many individual schools do, of course, draw up curriculum plans for each National Curriculum subject, though few that I have seen are based on any serious attempt to determine the order in which new concepts have to be mastered. The sensible thing would have been to do this planning nationally so that each school did not have to try to re-invent the wheel. But no, the cry went up that the National Curriculum was overburdened, which it was, and those who thought that the fact that teachers were being told what to teach was an attack on professionalism seized the opportunity to render the curriculum less 'prescriptive'. The vaguer, of course, the prescription, the greater the scope for 'professional' interpretation, but the greater, too, the burden on the individual teacher. Why have a National Curriculum if it can be interpreted in a different way by every school and teacher? We have probably reached the point where there is no point, and the Government might as well cave in completely to union demand and abolish the whole wretched thing.

This sorry saga is not, however, the immediate issue. If the Government has not done it, the school must. For pupil progress cannot be assessed if there is no concept of what progress entails. Ah, the objection will come, but you don't fatten a pig by weighing it. Indeed, you do not, but no teacher ever taught any child anything if they did not have a pretty clear idea of what the child knew and did not know. Children are not pigs and the curriculum they study is not, or ought not to be, swill. The lament that regular tests distress children is equally silly. If the teacher wants the child to be distressed, then, yes, it can be managed easily enough, but a low key, regular programme of testing never upset anyone. Schools that test regularly in fact avoid distress, the real distress that comes when pupils fall further and further behind their peers. Once again, sentimentality and silliness conspire to drive common sense out of the window and deliver yet more educational failure.

There is no point in identifying failure if nothing is to be done about it. Too often nothing is. This is one of the greatest weaknesses of English education. Once a child begins to fall behind, he is likely to fall further behind. It does not have to be like this. It is not in other countries and it should not be in England.

The immediate response will be that if classes were smaller it would not happen. But classes, as I have just explained, are never going to be small enough. The solution, assuming that progression in each subject has been articulated carefully and logically and that a regular system of diagnostic assessment is in place (two assumptions that we cannot make), is: (1) more extensive and more intelligent use of classroom assistants; (2) a greater acceptance of the fact that some children may take longer to master a concept than others and may, as a last resort, need to be kept down a year; (3) much more extensive use of what is known as 'peer tutoring'; and (4) better whole class teaching.

Assistants are now employed in many, particularly primary, classrooms. We have hardly, however, begun to exploit their potential and we would do well to invest some of the millions we are wasting on other initiatives, in employing many more. To be effective, the assistant must, of course, understand what, lesson by lesson, the teacher is trying to achieve. Equally, he or she must be able to see things from the pupil's point of view, to appreciate the steps in the argument that some pupils are going to find difficult. It is a matter of structuring the lesson to allow time for an assistant to work with an individual child or group of children to ensure that the new concept or skill has been mastered.

There is nothing radical in this suggestion. It already happens. What is needed now is the political commitment to launch a national recruitment and training campaign that offers those members of the public who want it a clear route through from being a classroom assistant to becoming a teacher. And, of course, a recognition that classroom assistants are, at present, paid a pittance. Once again, it is a matter of cutting back on new initiatives and headquarters staff in order to use taxpayers' money where it should be used and where it is going to make a real difference – in classrooms.

The suggestion that a child should not automatically progress from one year to the next is deeply counter-cultural. What, it will inevitably be asked, of the child's self-esteem? How could we be so cruel? The real question is how we can be so cruel as to put a child in a situation where he or she is bound to fail; why we tolerate an approach which means that, as each year goes by, some children know that they understand less and less. This is the real cruelty. In France where a significant number of pupils have repeated a year by the time they reach school leaving age, it is different. Perhaps we have something to learn.

'Peer-tutoring' has enormous potential. The idea could not be simpler: one pupil tutors another. It might be an older pupil. It might be one pupil tutoring another in the same class. It does not matter. The point is that the school has thought through how it can establish a programme in which pupils support each other to happen.

Last year I spent a fascinating day at the Sabis International School in Springfield, Massachusetts. A number of schools in England use peer-tutoring in a rather haphazard way, but none has made it as central and important a feature of teaching and learning as Sabis. Ninety-five per cent of the twelve hundred or so students in this school have made a voluntary commitment to what is called 'Student Life'. Student Life is a student body that shadows, as it were, the adult organisation of the school. It supports the teachers in the maintenance of discipline, in general administration, in running sporting and cultural activities, and, crucially, in academic learning. Students register the subject area in which they are competent and willing to tutor other students. Systems have been established to ensure that a student who has a problem can be put in touch with another who is prepared to help. Time is built into the school day to allow it to happen. It works. If I had not seen for myself and talked to students, I may well have been sceptical. As it is, this is one innovation that we ought, I believe, to be introducing into our schools.

But none of these strategies is going to have much impact if the quality of whole class teaching is not improved. This is my fifth and final traditional truth.

The academics argue, of course, that we need more research into what constitutes good teaching. Professor Di Bentley of Sheffield Hallam University believes that we must encourage the pursuit of a 'holistic problematised pedagogy'. Twelve million pounds of public money are spent each year on an Economic and Social Science Council project into effective teaching. When will we ever learn? Good teachers, as I have argued again and again in this book, are men and women who have a firm intellectual mastery of the subject they are teaching, high expectations of their pupils, and a confident grip on the craft of the classroom. They can, that is, keep discipline, explain things clearly, ask questions and respond to pupils' answers in a positive way, and so on. Immensely difficult though it is in practice to teach well, there is no intellectual mystique, no new discoveries which, given a huge investment of public funds, will transform what happens in classrooms across the land. Good teachers, as Jonathan Smith reminds us, tell you things. That should be the end of the story. The money currently wasted on research could then be invested in training that focuses on subject knowledge and pedagogic skills and helps teachers to teach more effectively.

The restoration of these simple traditional truths about teaching is the key to higher standards of pupil achievement and better teacher morale. The former, of course, leads to the latter. Teachers who work in successful schools do not whinge about the impossibility of their lot. Those, conversely, who know that they are not doing a very effective job are unlikely to enjoy particularly high professional self-esteem. The deeper their sense of failure, the greener the grass of other careers and the more desperate the desire to escape. It is a natural enough reaction, as is the tendency to rationalise the personal failure in terms of the general impossibility of the job. If we want higher morale, we must secure more effective teaching and more effective teaching means more traditional, whole class teaching.

IV

That said, the job for many teachers is, if not impossible, a lot less rational than it ought to be. The teacher unions and the General Teaching Council think that the most serious problem is the Government's failure to involve teachers in the development of new initiatives. It is not. It is, perm any combination: the failure of the headteacher to offer any kind of educational vision, or to ensure even basic order in the classrooms of his/her school; the presence in mainstream schools of children who cannot or will not accept the conventions of normal classroom behaviour; the burden of administration that adds nothing to a teacher's effectiveness in the classroom; and, last, but certainly not least in areas like London and the South-East where escalating house prices have made it harder and harder for teachers to find anywhere half decent to live, pay.

These are problems that could be solved. In fact, as everyone knows, the Government has chosen to make them worse.

OFSTED inspection evidence shows, as I said in Chapter 1, that three out of ten headteachers are failing to lead their schools effectively. You do not have to work in education to know what this means. Just think for a moment about the times when you have worked for a boss who was not up to the job, the frustration you felt at his reluctance to take a decision, his inability to remember what he (sort of) decided yesterday, his failure to grasp an issue, however simple and straightforward it might be, his cowardice when it came to confronting incompetence and inefficiency. We have all had bosses like that and we all know the impact they can have on our own morale and commitment. Teaching is a difficult, demanding job and teachers have a right to expect a headteacher who is there with them, prodding, cajoling, praising and, whatever he may do or say in private, supporting when pupils and their parents play up.

The Government recognises this. It decides that what it must do is set up a National College for School Leadership (NCSL), which sounds a brilliant idea, doesn't it? Well, it was not. The NCSL has existed now for just over a year. Next year it will have a budget of sixty million pounds. A number of well-meaning people have scurried hither and thither talking to leaders across the country, across the public and private sectors, across, no doubt, the world. The result? A report from the NCSL 'think tank' that is a classic example of the failure of the educational establishment to think. It proudly rehearses every possible platitude on the knowledge society, 'active' pupil learning and, indeed, leadership itself. It is written in a pompous and convoluted style that renders the simplest, most commonsensical proposition meaningless. As a blue print for the NCSL's programme of work it is, quite simply, a disaster.

Here, to give you a flavour, are some extracts from the Ten Propositions about Leadership for Transforming Learning that are offered to us. 'Taken together' these ten propositions 'constitute the parameters for a framework for school leadership that is firmly grounded in learning as well as transformational'. Pause for a moment. Reread this sentence. If the word 'transformational' (like, in my case, 'holistic') triggers an immediate cringe, repress it. Just ask yourself whether you have any idea what the sentence means. Ask yourself whether the author had any idea. To be fair, the next paragraph provides a gloss. 'The emphasis on transformation is both deliberate and necessary'. Why? Because 'reform strategies and leadership programmes can no longer take only an incremental approach to change to student and learning'. Again, pause. So change is no longer a matter of planning one improvement after another, thinking through how next term you can build on the achievements of this? No, stupid. That is old hat. What we have now is an 'ambitious national agenda for sustainable improvement for all students in all settings'. Note here the you-would-have-thought redundant 'sustainable', but note more the fact that the ambitions of our national politicians are so intensely demanding that headteachers must respond immediately and, it goes without saying, doesn't it, transformatively. The national agenda is imposed upon the school agenda and a head who makes a realistic assessment of what and just how much can be taken on at any given moment is not, apparently, the kind of leader we now want.

Leadership, moreover, 'has to be seen within a whole school or systems context and to impact both on classroom practice and the work culture of the school'. Indeed it does. That is what I always thought heads were paid to do: to raise standards in classrooms and make sure that the school as an organisation functioned smoothly and positively. Perhaps this is what the Think Tank means? But perhaps not, for given this new-millennium speak it is often hard to know what is meant.

So, too, with the ten propositions. School leadership must:

- be purposeful, inclusive and values driven
- embrace the distinctive and individual context of the school
- promote an active view of learning
- be instructionally focused
- be a function that is dispersed throughout the school community
- build capacity by developing the school as a learning community
- be futures oriented and strategically driven

Enough, I cannot bear to type all ten. Has anyone ever thought that leadership should be purposeless, that it should exclude children or members of staff or parents, that it can be value-less? You might be wondering about the 'embrace'. I can help. This means that leadership must 'audit its stakeholder expectations, recognising and assessing the multiple levels of the school – community, parents, students, teachers and governors, behavioural, attitudinal, cognitive and relational variables'. So now you know. And on and on it goes. We cannot teach a quarter of primary school children to read and this Think Tank has the arrogance and stupidity to write: 'Leadership to promote student learning needs to give attention to engaging students and parents as active participants, and expanding the teaching and learning repertoires of teachers and students respectively'. It is twaddle. It would be comic if it were not for the fact that this is the 'world class', multi-million pound initiative the Government has invented to ensure that we have the leadership in our schools our teachers need if they are to do their job.

Then there are the disruptive pupils. As I have said, it is twenty-five years since I taught, but I can still remember my own feelings on leaving a classroom where I knew that I had failed the majority because I had had to devote ninety per cent of my time and energy to the two or three who were determined to cause mayhem. It was not just or even primarily the fact that the struggle to contain disruptive behaviour is psychologically and physically exhausting. What really hurt is the sense of, first, failure because I knew that I had done nothing for the children who had wanted to learn; second, frustration, because I knew I had had no alternative; and, third, despair, because I knew that the next lesson was likely to be much the same if not worse.

Typically, the lesson would begin well only to be disrupted after five minutes or so. The deviant two or three would swagger in causing maximum mayhem as they progressed through the classroom to vacant seats on the back row. Sometimes, I would insist that they sat apart at the front of the class, but the battle was not really worth the torrent of abuse it would inevitably inspire. The better, if humiliating, strategy was to wheedle and cajole in the hope that some semblance of peace and quiet could be engineered for part, at least, of the lesson.

Those young men and women I can remember so well should not have been in my English lessons. They were uncontrollable. It was not just me. Other members of staff found them equally difficult. You would have thought, twenty-five years on, that our political masters might have learnt. David Blunkett's insistence when he was Secretary of State that headteachers should bend over backwards not to exclude difficult pupils caused untold harm. Estelle Morris has now reversed this policy and made it clear that headteachers have the right to decide whether or not, in the interests of the majority, a pupil should be excluded. The headteacher is still, however, in a very difficult position. Understandably enough, they see exclusion as a final and very regrettable step. The problem is that we do not have enough alternative provision for those who are excluded. A sensible government would expand the quantity and raise the quality of such provision as an immediate priority. There is still, despite the fact that common sense has begun to dawn, a very long way to go.

Ms Morris ought also to do everything in her power to speed up the introduction of vocational and work-based training and apprenticeships announced in last year's White Paper on the future of secondary education. Exasperated as I so often was by the behaviour of my unteachable students, I could, sitting in the White Hart after a pint or two of restorative bitter, see things from their point of view. They had given up a long time ago. Illiterate and innumerate, they knew that they could not compete with their more academic peers. They knew that they would be lucky to scramble together a handful of low-level CSEs. They sought, therefore, refuge in loutishness, and who can blame them? The more outrageous their behaviour, the more notorious their reputation. Notoriety might not be much, but it is better than the open ridicule they might otherwise have received from their peers.

The Government could, similarly, do a great deal to ease the burden of unproductive, unnecessary administration that exhausts teachers before they even set forth in the classroom. There is only one question to ask of any new initiative. Does it help a teacher to teach better? If the answer is yes, then the effort involved in its implementation is justified. If no, forget it. Few recent initiatives, apart from the National Literacy and Numeracy Strategies, have passed this test. Few, on the evidence of the Key Stage 3 strategy which is intended to 'transform' teaching in the early years of secondary education, are likely to do so in future. Politicians, desperate for a quick fix and anxious to be seen to be doing something, will not admit it, but it is consolidation we need now, not the latest bright idea from the Standards and Effectiveness or Innovation Units.

Local education authorities are, however, equally to blame. Too many have seized on national initiatives as a justification for their own existence, over-complicating what are already labyrinthine arrangements. Some, like Birmingham, continue to launch their own strategies for raising standards, confident that they can do it better than anyone else and indifferent to the number of balls their headteachers are already having to juggle. Others insist, despite the fact that their schools are inspected by OFSTED, on mounting their own evaluations of different kinds. There are LEAs that understand that schools can only do so much at once and that their job is to provide high quality and cost-effective back-up support, but sadly they are very much in the minority.

The strong headteacher will defend his staff from all this bureaucratic zeal. I am well aware that it is an easy thing for an ex-Chief Inspector to say, but the head has to have the courage of his convictions and define his own agenda. To juggle too many balls is to invite disaster. It may well be that the Government's priority, literacy, for example, is the school's. If it is not, then the LEA adviser, or, for that matter, the OFSTED inspector, must be told that the 'priority' will be examined in due course when the governing body is confident that current developments have been concluded satisfactorily.

Weak headteachers, understandably, find this hard. Less understandably, they fill the diary with meeting after meeting – desperate, I suppose, to postpone the horror of having to take a decision. They demand that their teachers write policies on every conceivable aspect of school life so that, when the inspector calls, they can hide behind the pile of paper. They require their teachers to document each lesson, to set out, often in ridiculous detail, aims and objectives and to review, after the event, how it all went. Do not misinterpret me. Preparation is vital and teachers ought to think about the strengths and weaknesses of the lessons they teach. What we do not need is documentation for the sake of documentation: paperwork that is produced in order to cover the headteacher's backside. There is far too much of it at the moment, and it is headteachers, not the Secretary of State, who are responsible. We need more leadership.

Finally, in the quest to understand why teaching is an unattractive career for many bright graduates, there is pay. Nobody ever went into teaching for the money, and nobody ever will. Like everyone else, however, teachers have to live, and it has become virtually impossible for young teachers to live in areas where property prices are so high. Once the rent or the mortgage has been paid, there is little left. The Government seems to think that the answer is a 'golden hello'. It is not. Starting salaries are, in fact, not that bad. What is needed is a fundamental re-think of the whole salary structure so that students who are contemplating teaching as a career know that, if they are any good, they can earn substantially more than is currently possible.

If they are any good: the Government must admit that the current performance pay scheme is a debacle. Performance pay means an annual appraisal against objectives, not a once in a career 'threshold' appraisal that guarantees you the extra pay, irrespective of your commitment and achievement, for life. The unions will, of course, resist, but so be it. The culture of teaching has to be changed so that the brightest and the best receive their just rewards.

Neither can we go on pretending that a national pay scale is sustainable. Schools in areas of high housing cost must be able to pay their teachers more. This means a national funding formula for schools that delivers a higher budget to schools in the South East and other similar areas where teachers cannot, at present, afford to live. There is a second problem. Teachers of some subjects, like mathematics or physics, are desperately difficult to recruit. We cannot go on bucking basic laws of supply and demand. These teachers are going to have to be paid more. The reaction of teachers of other subjects will for understandable reasons be difficult to manage, but there is no alternative. We have to move from nationally determined salary arrangements that give headteachers precious little room for manoeuvre to a situation in which schools are given a budget that reflects their geographical situation and heads and governing bodies have the management autonomy to take the remuneration decisions that make sense in their particular circumstance.

There is no magic wand. It is hard, given the fact that fewer and fewer students choose to study mathematics and science at university, to see how shortages in these subjects are ever going to be resolved. The problem is that we are locked in a vicious circle. The more difficult it is to recruit good teachers in these subjects, the less likely it is that future generations of students will be inspired to read mathematics and science. Year by year, the pool for recruitment becomes smaller. That said, the action I have outlined would help. The Government should stop flailing around inventing new recruitment wheezes. It should stop wasting public money on what must be a hugely expensive advertising campaign (there were three advertisements, one full page, in the *Sunday Times*, on the weekend I wrote this chapter). Deal with disruptive children. Cut the paperwork and the distractions. Reform the approach to pay. Action on these fronts would, at the very least, ease the current crisis.

CHAPTER 4

OFSTED

The question was one I had been asked hundreds, if not thousands of times before: 'Mr Woodhead, how can you justify a system of school inspection which is demoralising the entire teaching profession?'. The interviewer paused for effect before adding a personal anecdote. 'I have', she said, 'many friends who are teachers. They are terrified at the prospect of inspectors sitting in the back of their lessons in order to judge their effectiveness. The whole life of the school stops for weeks in the run-up to an inspection. Scores of documents have to be written to satisfy the bureaucratic demands. It is a nightmare, a total nightmare'. It was not the most impartial of radio interviews, but it was pretty typical.

The basic facts are these. All schools have to be inspected once within a maximum of six years. The size and length of the inspection is, as you would expect, determined by the size of the school. A very small primary school might be visited by a couple of inspectors for a couple of days; twenty or more inspectors will be involved in the inspection of a large comprehensive school. OFSTED asks only for documents that the school should possess. One of the first things I did as Chief Inspector was to consult with the teacher unions about how the demands for paperwork could be cut down. 'There is often an inverse correlation', I used to say at headteachers' conferences, 'between the amount of documentation a school supplies to the inspectors and the quality of what really matters: the teaching and learning inspectors observe in the classroom'. I meant it. I have always criticised the bureaucratic obsession with plans and records. Policies on, for example, discipline and how the school is going to meet the requirements of different National Curriculum subjects are, of course, vital. But the demands, generated by LEAs and central government, have in recent years become ridiculous. OFSTED might be an easy scapegoat, but it is not the culprit.

During an inspection a teacher will, typically, have two or three of her lessons observed. It will vary from teacher to teacher and in primary schools the average is slightly more, but this is a typical figure. Three lessons every six years? An hour and a half with an inspector in the back of your classroom? An inspector who knows that he must do all he can to put the teacher at her ease. Most teachers will, of course, feel a bit anxious. Nobody likes having their performance in a job evaluated and the most conscientious are likely to be the most anxious. But performance review is now the norm in pretty well all jobs. As, of course, it should be. If teachers could demonstrate that inspection was unjustifiably burdensome and oppressive then they would have a case. They cannot and they have not.

It is worth remembering, too, that the most likely outcome is that the inspector will tell the teacher or headteacher that he or she is doing a good job. As Chief Inspector, I would from time to time receive letters from headteachers who wanted me to know how much the positive comments made by inspectors meant to them and their staff. 'I've been a head for twelve years', one wrote, 'and nobody has ever taken a serious look at what I'm doing. Nobody has ever told me that I'm doing a good job. We have had excellent coverage in the local paper and all the parents are saying how wonderful it is. It is hard to tell you what our report has done for my morale – and my colleagues are over the moon'. So much, I can remember thinking as I read this letter, for the allegation that OFSTED inspectors only wanted to find fault and that I personally was determined to pillory and humiliate every teacher across the land. I am confident that an objective review of the 40,000 inspection reports OFSTED has now published would reveal that the good news far outweighs the bad.

'That's fine', you might be thinking. 'Everybody is happy when the school is judged to be successful. It must, though, be a different story when the inspector sits down with the headteacher and tells him that his school has real problems?' Such conversations can, I agree, be very difficult. Most heads are, understandably, upset. Some are devastated. Some simply cannot come to terms with the judgement.

Years before I had anything to do with the national inspectorate, when I was still working in an LEA, I had to find a way to remove a headteacher from one of the authority's schools. Standards in the school were low and getting worse. There was a great deal of staff unhappiness and, unsurprisingly, the school had become so unpopular with parents that its roll was declining dramatically. The situation had deteriorated to the point where urgent action was needed. The head would not accept that the school, because of his lack of leadership, was in crisis. He had been ill, and his illness had, perhaps, affected his judgement. He certainly hid behind it, alternately proffering it as an excuse and arguing that now he was on the mend all would be well. As is so often the case, it was everybody else's fault. He had some very weak staff, the Authority had not been supportive, a number of the governors had never wanted him appointed and were now out to get rid of him. In the end, after a great deal of discussion and mutual angst, I persuaded him to go, and he retired on ill health with a very good package. If he had stayed in post, the pressure of the job may well have killed him. Has he ever come to realise that, painful though the experience was at the time, his early retirement might just have been in his interests as well as the school's? No, he has not. Every now and again, I still receive bitter, angry letters attacking me for my failure to back him in his time of need.

It is not easy for anyone. Good can and does, however, come out of these traumatic events. Back in 1996 I visited a large comprehensive school in the North-East that had just come out of the failed school category. I walked round with the headteacher, visiting classrooms, talking to children and their teachers. I was extremely impressed. 'Look', the head said to me afterwards as we had a cup of coffee in his office, 'I have taught in this school for twenty years. I was deputy at the time of the inspection. I would not have admitted it to you then, but we were complacent. We knew that we were drifting, that the kids should have been achieving more, but none of us had the energy, the determination, to do anything about it. We did not realise how bad things were. Yes, of course, the news that we were actually a failing school was a dreadful shock. Initially, I was furious. They were right, though, those inspectors, and everything that has happened since has been because of what they said and wrote. Who knows? We might have got round to doing something. No doubt, we would have done in due course. But things would not have changed so quickly and dramatically. We've moved heaven and earth to get out of the failed school category. These kids are realising their potential and we as a staff feel better about what we are doing than we have for years'. That school was well on the way to recovery. Other schools that failed their inspection are now extremely successful. One, Urchfont School in Wiltshire, is now the most successful primary schools in the country: number one in last year's league table. Failing the inspection was the best thing that ever happened to this school, the Chair of the Governors told me when I visited.

It will be dismissed out of hand by those who oppose inspection, but this headteacher's comment is the other side of the inspection coin. 'We do not like inspection', he said to me at a conference in Suffolk a couple of months before I resigned. 'Of course we don't. Who would? In public we'll moan and groan, but in private most of us agree that the vast majority of OFSTED inspectors do a good, professional job. We recognise that inspection is essential. Every now and again we need that external challenge and it is right that we are accountable to the communities we serve'.

This was precisely the thinking behind the creation of OFSTED. When I started teaching in 1969, schools were left very much to manage their own business. Parents had their annual meeting with the teachers who taught their children and that was that. Few, if any, LEAs inspected their schools. A primary school, the perhaps apocryphal story goes, could expect an HMI inspection every two hundred and fifty years. Since in most parts of the country the Eleven Plus had been abolished, nobody had the faintest idea what was happening in the primary sector. The situation was marginally better in the secondary sector in that examination statistics told us something about what the system as a whole was achieving, but this overview was no use to a parent trying to decide which was the best school for their child. The school curriculum, moreover, in a phrase popular at the time, was 'a secret garden': the jealously guarded province of the educational expert who tended to dismiss lay questions or expressions of concern as an unwarranted intrusion into what ought, the argument went, to be an exclusively professional domain.

If state education had been achieving the results parents, politicians and businessmen wanted, none of this might have mattered. It was not. In 1976, Jim Callaghan had dared to suggest that all was not well with the nation's schools. We had, however, to wait until 1988 for any serious programme of reform. Since then hardly a year has passed without some piece of legislation affecting education, but it was the Education Reform Act of 1988 which saw the introduction of the National Curriculum and its associated tests and the Education (Schools) Act of 1992 which paved the way for the creation of OFSTED that changed the world of education for good.

My Suffolk headteacher felt that teachers have now accepted accountability as an uncomfortable, but necessary fact of life. I am not so sure. The teacher unions certainly continue to oppose both performance tables and inspection. They state, disingenuously, that 'in principle' they support the latter, but in fact argue that schools should be free to evaluate their own performance. Forgetful of the cliché that trust has to be earned and oblivious to the fact that standards in schools remain too low, they repeatedly complain that we are not prepared to trust our teachers.

There is, I am afraid, a way still to go before the teaching profession as a whole acknowledges that, as publicly funded institutions, schools must be open to public scrutiny.

Parents, on the other hand, have, by and large, welcomed OFSTED. Some, inevitably, have been influenced by the black propaganda spun by the teacher unions. Occasionally, parents who have children in a school that fails its inspection cannot believe the judgement and side with the teachers. 'How dare you', they ask incredulously, 'criticise that nice Miss Jones?'. But generally, for very obvious reasons, they like the fact that they now know what is going on in the schools their children attend or might attend.

A year or so after I had been appointed to OFSTED, *Panorama* made a documentary about school inspection. The scene that sticks in my mind is that of a mum talking about how she had known that her son was not making the progress he should. She had gone to the school to discuss her concerns, but had been fobbed off, she felt, with a load of platitudes. The school was then inspected and the report picked up problems in her son's class. Armed with this evidence, she went back and tackled the head again. This time he had to concede that all might not be well. It was a nice example of the impotence and frustration parents can sometimes feel and of how an OFSTED inspection can help the consumer put his or her case.

As Chief Inspector, I always felt that the parent was our main audience and our contribution to this new transparency our greatest achievement. My senior colleagues in OFSTED tended to disagree. They were more concerned with the contribution we were or were not making to school improvement than they were with the provision of hard information to parents. Hence, I suppose, the strapline, invented before my appointment: 'Improvement through inspection'. Most teachers and many MPs took the same view. What mattered was what the teacher felt, not what the parents wanted. The Education Select Committee, particularly under Barry Shearman's chairmanship, was, for instance, obsessed with teacher reaction to OFSTED. Or, to put it more accurately, it identified (with one or two honourable exceptions) with the anxieties felt by more insecure members of the profession and was all too ready to believe the scare stories promulgated by the unions.

Whenever I appeared before the committee, Mr Shearman acted as if he were an impartial chairman. It was not, in my judgement, a convincing performance. I have no idea what he said to headteachers when he spoke at their conferences, but, having listened to him once or twice on the radio, I can imagine.

'The last thing we want is a Witchfinder General stomping up and down the land terrifying teachers', he thundered one Saturday morning on the *Today* programme. I was, as it happened, wending my innocent way down the Euston Road. I was so surprised that I stopped the car and phoned the *Today* studio and asked them to play their recording back to me. They did. I had not been dreaming. Given that the Prime Minister had always gone out of his way to praise OFSTED's contribution, I have, I suppose, to admire Mr Shearman's independence of spirit. I cannot say, though, that I ever had much confidence in his impartiality as the chairman of the Commons Committee to which from time to time I had the misfortune to have to report.

Mr Shearman's committee was, however, an irrelevance. It should not have been, but it was. As a public servant, I fully accepted that I should be accountable to Parliament through the committee. The principle was absolutely right. The practice was not. This was a committee that more often than not could not be bothered to do its homework. The prejudices and egos of its members made it difficult to have any serious debate. In a session which was meant to be about the Ofsted Annual Report on the performance of English Schools, I was, for example, suddenly asked by Evan Harris whether I was homophobic. I was taken to task for daring to exceed my brief and comment on academic standards in Higher Education. Nobody on the committee seemed remotely interested in whether I, and umpteen academics, were right to express concerns. So, too, with A levels. Nobody was prepared to face up to the fact that these examinations had changed very significantly over the years, and, as a consequence, may have become easier. Nobody wanted to discuss the difficulties university admission tutors were experiencing now that so many candidates were gaining A or B grades. The committee simply wanted to prove that I did not have the evidence for something I had not in fact said. I was, it seemed, a dangerous maverick who had to be nailed. What should have been an opportunity to discuss serious educational issues degenerated into a ritual of increasingly rancorous confrontation in which I was attacked for doing what Parliament required me to do.

For Parliament was clear. OFSTED was to report without fear or favour. If there were problems in our schools, then these problems must be brought out into the open. Why else was OFSTED established? My ex HMI colleagues will not like me saying it, but there was more than a grain of truth in the accusation that HMI (the national inspectorate before OFSTED was created in 1992) had, like the proverbial dog, failed to bark in the night. Parents knew what was happening. Employers had been complaining for years. Nothing had happened. The juggernaut had ground on. Nothing and nobody, it seemed, could dent the self-confidence and complacency of the educational establishment. HMI should have blown the whistle and they did not.

OFSTED was created to challenge the producer interest, and that, for better or worse, is what, under my leadership, it did. I did not set out to seek confrontation for confrontation's sake. Our job, as I saw it, was to gather the facts and then to make sure that their significance was understood by everyone who had an interest in our schools. If this upset some academics and politicians, then my attitude was, frankly, so be it. Controversy was unavoidable, and, in that it focused media and public attention on what had happened to state education, desirable. The educational establishment was bound, after all, to defend its discredited thinking and ineffective practices. It was, I suppose, inevitable, if at the time dispiriting, that Labour MPs, unwilling or unable to ponder the sentimentality of the policies they espoused with such impressive rhetorical fervour, would reduce the debate to party political knockabout.

Was it wrong to point out that 4 per cent of teachers were not, on the inspection evidence, up to the job? That one in ten headteachers was judged to be an ineffective leader? That, when we surveyed fifty inner-London primary schools, we found appallingly low levels of literacy and numeracy? That Hackney, Islington, Waltham Forest, Leeds and Bradford LEAs (to name but five) were shambolic in their provision of services to schools? To bring the problem out into the open is to force those responsible – be it the headteacher, the Chief Education Officer or the Secretary of State – to find a solution. To sweep it under the carpet is to compound the misery of the children the system fails, and, equally, to undermine the credibility of everyone who works in state education. Everyone – for the good teacher, school and LEA is tarred by the indiscriminate brush of local gossip and media criticism. If the teaching profession wants a better press, a more positive image and higher public esteem, it must recognise that the wounds that have festered for too long must be cleansed.

There is, in fact, no conflict between OFSTED's responsibility to expose failure and its commitment to contribute to school improvement. The latter depends on the intelligence and integrity which is brought to bear on the former. This is true at the level of the individual school and the system as a whole. As of December, 1303 schools have failed their inspection. Many of these have become successful, over-subscribed schools. Would these schools be successful if they had not failed? Perhaps, but I somehow doubt it. As the headteacher I quoted a page or two back admitted, the inspection and the subsequent trauma of failure was the catalyst his school needed to tackle its problems. The most important examples of the contribution inspection has made at the national level are the literacy and numeracy strategies. It was the inspection evidence gathered in those inner-London primary schools that persuaded Gillian Shephard to introduce the strategies. 75 per cent and 71 per cent of eleven-year-olds now reach the national standard in English and Mathematics respectively. There is a long way still to go, but the last four years has seen dramatic progress. Again, I very much doubt that it would have happened without OFSTED.

I also believe that inspection can, and in some cases does, help headteachers of successful schools. The longer you do a job, in my experience, the harder it is to maintain an objective, fresh perspective on the strengths and weaknesses of the organisation in which you work. I would add, too, that the more senior you are in the organisation the more likely it is that you will kid yourself. The decisions have, if you are in charge, been yours. There is nobody else to blame for the mistakes and it is tempting to pretend that the situation is healthier than it is. No doubt some people find it easier to remain detached than I did, but any chief executive or headteacher who believes that he has his finger on every strength and every weakness in his firm or school is living in a fantasy world.

In principle, therefore, the fresh perspective of the inspection team ought to be of real value. In practice, it depends, obviously enough, on two things: the intelligence of the team, and the receptivity of the head and his senior management. I couldn't put my hand on my heart and say that every OFSTED report published in my time sparkled with helpful insight. Too many, if I am honest, were dull, were written very much to a formula, and were unlikely, therefore, to contribute much of value to a headteacher's thinking.

A headteacher who received such a report should, I once said, throw it in the nearest wastepaper bin. The audience found it funny and the *Times Educational Supplement* made predictable mischief. It was not, however, a joke. If 'improvement through inspection' was the goal, then our reports had to be not just good, but first rate: sharp, rigorous, analytical, clear and convincing in their argument and their deployment of evidence.

Too many in my time were not. Too many, I suspect, are still not. OFSTED is not therefore making the contribution it should to progress in our more effective schools.

But, if the quality of the report is crucial, then so, too, is the attitude of the headteacher. The more able the headteacher, the more likely it is that the report will be given serious consideration. Weak, insecure headteachers tend, as you would expect, either to dismiss negative comments out of hand or to complain that they already knew about the problem and were doing all they could to tackle it. 'The report', they will complain, 'told me nothing I didn't know already'. Perhaps it did not. Perhaps it was one of our inadequate reports. But, then again, I used to think when headteachers stood up at conferences to deliver this sort of smug statement, perhaps you are as self-righteous and self-deluding as you sound. I never had the courage to say it. I regret that.

Aggrieved headteachers were not, as everyone knows, the only ones who wanted to take a pot at OFSTED. The fact that most headteachers were satisfied with their inspection was an irrelevance. So, too, was the evidence that inspection was having a positive impact both on individual schools, and, through the advice we gave to ministers, the system as a whole. Hardly a week went by in the six years I was Chief Inspector without some horror headline or critical article. I was accused of 'politicising' the inspection process. Our whole approach was said to be methodologically flawed and the evidence we gathered was, therefore, dismissed as worthless. We were, and this was the most heartfelt criticism of all, demoralising the entire teaching profession. Our punitive and hostile approach, it was alleged, was driving teachers in their droves into as early a retirement as they could arrange.

Did I? Was it? Were we? It will surprise nobody if I plead not guilty on all three charges. Does it matter, anyway? To me, perhaps, a little, but not actually that much. I have never found it difficult, having left a job, to turn my mind to the new challenge. It is history certainly. We now have a different, determinedly teacher friendly OFSTED. The past is the past, gone. The debate, however, about the role of the inspectorate continues and there are lessons to be learnt from the story of OFSTED's first few turbulent years. Some response, however partial, is needed.

Let's start with the 'politicisation' jibe. Those who wanted the world to believe that OFSTED had become, in Tony Mooney's rather witty phrase, 'the para-military wing of the DFEE', liked to pretend that HMI had been independent of government. It had not. 'Never at any point in its history was HMI wholly or constitutionally independent of government'. That is Eric Bolton speaking and, as the last HMCI before OFSTED was established, he ought to know. What, moreover, does the accusation that OFSTED has been politicised really mean? Answer: the Conservative Government of the day was, it was said, hostile to state education and wanted bullets to fire, OFSTED had criticised some teachers and some schools, OFSTED must, therefore, be dancing to the tune of its political masters.

Ignore the logic, or, rather, lack of logic. What is interesting here is the assumption that the inspectorate has to take sides. There was a moment during the selection process that led to my appointment as Chief Inspector when the headhunter with whom I was chatting shifted in his chair. He looked me in the eye and the tone of the conversation shifted a gear. 'Suppose you get this job', he said, 'would you see yourself as the voice of the profession, the man whose responsibility it is to speak out on behalf of teachers?' 'No', I can remember replying, 'I would not. The Chief Inspector has to be independent. When necessary he must be able to criticise both teachers and government. He cannot afford to be too close to either constituency. His responsibility is to parents, the local communities schools serve, and, ultimately, to children'. He scribbled furiously, but did not reply. Afterwards, reflecting on the interview, it struck me that a lot probably rode on this little exchange.

It did. I learnt later that officials from the Department of Education, as it was then called, were none too happy that my answer had not told against me. I can understand their anxiety. Prior to the creation of OFSTED, HMCI had been a member of the Permanent Secretary's senior management board, working with other civil servants to an agreed agenda. The Department had been able to draw upon the Inspectorate's expertise and influence, if not determine, what it said and did not say. In 1992 Parliament had made OFSTED constitutionally independent. OFSTED was a government department, far smaller, of course, than the Department of Education, but, theoretically, on an equal footing. HMCI was its non-ministerial head and did not have to seek the Secretary of State's approval for his day-to-day actions. Civil servants like to be in control. It is ironic, given the accusation that under my leadership OFSTED danced to the Government's tune, but the truth is that the last thing officials wanted was for an outsider like me to be appointed to a position where they could not pull the strings.

The 'politicisation' charge might have been silly, but the issue underlying it was and is very important. In 1992, Parliament decided, rightly in my view, that the inspectorate should be independent of the Secretary of State and the Department of Education. OFSTED was established as a non-ministerial government department with, in theory at least, its own budget and a Chief Inspector who was his own man. In practice, the DfES continues to hold the purse strings. Officials and politicians alike seek to exert influence over the supposedly independent inspectorate in a variety of ways. Conor Ryan, who was David Blunkett's press guru, would phone me up, for

example, to offer ever-so-nicely, in his soft Irish brogue, sugges-
tions as to what might be included or changed in speeches and
reports. Michael Barber, the then head of the Standards and
Effectiveness Unit at the DfES, would express his disappointment if we were to criticise one of his cherished initiatives.
David Blunkett himself would on occasion fire over a terse little
letter. Great care was taken, of course, not to overstep the mark,
but it was pretty clear which side felt that they should be calling
the shots.

'Side': I can hear the snort of disbelief now. 'There he goes
again. Prickly, confrontational, arrogant, incapable of working
with anyone'. Yes, that is me. But it is what the Chief Inspector
has to be if OFSTED is to maintain any semblance of independence. It was not easy and it never will be.

That, of course, is my version of events. The counter com-
plaint voiced most vociferously by the Select Committee, was
that the Chief Inspector was too bloody independent. To whom,
they asked, is he accountable? It is a good question. To the
Prime Minister, I suppose, as the head of a government department. To Parliament, through the Select Committee. To the
world and his wife through the media. The line to the PM is
problematic because it infringes the independence. The media
has teeth, but can only snarl. The Committee tried to snarl, but
was too comic to intimidate.

There is no satisfactory answer. 'Independence' is a concept
like that of 'partnership' that makes people feel good. An 'independent Inspectorate'? Yes, of course, everyone says, absolutely
essential. Schools must be inspected and the Secretary of State
can only benefit from impartial advice. In theory, it is fine. In
practice, of course, people do not like it. Politicians, if anything,
are more sensitive than headteachers. Their profile is higher,
their position far more insecure. Turbulent priests are not good
news. The relationship between the Chief Inspector of Schools

and ministers ought never to be easy. When it is, something is wrong.

With luck, there will be mutual respect. Personalities aside, it would however, help, if the Secretary of State's involvement in the appointment and management of the Chief Inspector were to be ended. At present, the Secretary of State decides who he wants and passes the name up the line to the PM. Given my relationship with Mr Shearman and his committee, it galls me to say it, but it would be better if the decision were to be made by the Select Committee on behalf of Parliament. It would be better, too, if the Chief Inspector's performance was appraised by the Cabinet Secretary and not the Permanent Secretary in the DfES. Such changes would not eliminate the potential for conflict. Nor should they. They would, however, strengthen the Chief Inspector's position, and, difficult though it might on occasion be for ministers, constitutionally this would be a good thing.

But only, of course, if we can trust the judgements made by OFSTED's inspectors. Can we? Professor Carol Taylor Fitzgibbon of Durham University does not think we can. 'A few observations of a rather small sample of a year's lessons' are not, in her view, 'an adequate base for judgement'. An OFSTED report is not, she thinks, worth the paper upon which it is written. 'Presented with the impossible task of wandering round the school and making judgements about effectiveness, inspectors', she argues, 'have traditionally grasped at straws'.

Most teachers will tell you that inspectors do not wander aimlessly about. They work to a very carefully drawn up schedule in which the criteria to be used in coming to judgements have been defined with extreme care. It is not just me that thinks this. Headteachers might not like inspection, but most agree that the Handbook for Inspection that sets out what inspectors do is an impressive document. Martin Roberts, for example, head of Cherwell School, Oxford, described it as:

One of the best official education publications of the last decade. While extremely thorough (dauntingly so at first sight) it is clear and sensible. Most important of all, the evaluative criteria it lays down by which inspectors must judge a school's performance are explicit. They relate where appropriate to a pupil's progress in learning and are plainly the distillation of years of intelligent analysis of what makes good schools.

I do not for one moment pretend that these criteria have been framed with such limpid clarity as to ensure that they are interpreted in exactly the same way by every inspector. Indeed, as I admitted in an earlier chapter, my single biggest doubt about OFSTED stems from the fact that some inspectors are unwilling or unable to jettison their progressive educational views. This is certainly a serious issue. The Handbook has, however, done a great deal to eliminate unacceptable idiosyncrasy of judgement. Remember, too, that nobody can work as an inspector until they have been trained and have proved they are up to the job. OFSTED monitors inspectors regularly and has acted swiftly when an inspector is, for whatever reason, failing to follow the instructions of the Handbook. Neither is Professor Fitzgibbon right to suggest that judgements are based solely on the observation of a few lessons. Inspectors study a sample of pupils' work and analyse test and examination data going back over the years to place the evidence they gather from classroom observation in a wider context. And, if the school is thought to be failing, the judgement has to be corroborated by a second HMI inspection.

If Professor Fitzgibbon were right, OFSTED would receive a great deal more complaints than it does. The inspection process is not fundamentally flawed in the way she suggests. It might well present too optimistic a view of what is happening in schools, but the approach is much more reliable and consistent than critics like Fitzgibbon would have us believe.

What, though, of the most fundamental criticism? 'In medieval Europe', wrote Chris Tipple when he was Chief Education Officer in Northumberland, 'it was witches. In late twentieth-century Britain it looks like failing teachers'. Is inspection, as a National Association of Schoolmasters and Union of Women Teachers (NASUWT) member once put it to me, 'a ritual of public humiliation'? Are OFSTED inspectors, in the dichotomy of the day, 'judgemental and punitive' when they should be 'developmental and supportive'? Are they demoralising the profession, driving teachers into an early retirement, or, in one or two well publicised cases, an early grave? Is the rhetoric of 'improvement through inspection' a sick joke? The unions and the liberal commentators and a fair sprinkling, perhaps a majority, of Labour and Liberal Democrat MPs are unanimous: 'Yes', they shout, 'it is all true. Thank God you have gone and a new conciliatory era has dawned'.

I repeat: a teacher is likely to be observed teaching for an hour and a half or so every four to six years. The inspector is under instruction to do all he can to defuse the anxiety. More often than not, the outcome of the inspection is reassuring. What we have here is either a cynical campaign to arouse political and public anxiety to a point where the nation rises up against the wickedness of OFSTED or a curious phenomena of group paranoia. I suspect it is a little bit of both, with the former feeding off the latter.

Given the facts I have just quoted, what do you make of a Professor of Education who describes inspection as a 'disruptive inquisition' involving 'extreme disturbance', who writes of the 'mental cruelty' inflicted on teachers who have been 'shattered' by the experience, who quotes an 'independent consultant' as saying 'I am a shoulder to cry on and believe me they cry'.

How do you respond to another professor who sees teachers as 'marginalised victims' driven to the brink by a government which has demolished 'the very professional cultures of teaching upon which the whole reform edifice should have been built'. Or to this testimony from the front line, the reaction of a headteacher who received, believe it or not, a *good* OFSTED report:

> For the first couple of months after OFSTED our momentum kept going. We were keen to become the perfect model in our vision. But then we crashed – exhaustion and the knowledge that we were not superhuman. With Christmas came awareness of another life. I cooked a meal for my family for the first time in a year. Two teachers, unwell before Christmas, have not returned to school. Two teachers out of eight of us, one being deputy head.

It is, as I have recognised, the most dedicated who worry the most. But the question has to be asked: is there not something wrong when an ex headteacher reacts in this way? Wrong not with the inspection process, but, if this is a representative response, with the whole culture of teaching? The problem, of course, is that the more such letters are published and discussed, the more the elders of the tribe proclaim the punitive horror and injustice of it all, the more the mythology grows. A natural anxiety escalates into a neurosis. Teachers read that they have become 'marginalised victims' and some come to feel that they are. The headlines create the very despondency they trumpet.

Rarely, if ever, are the accusations substantiated. Take Stuart Maclure, an ex-editor of the *Times Educational Supplement*, a grand old man of the tribe who really ought to know better:

The fundamental truth remains that the teachers in schools are the only teachers there are to do the job, and their competence and confidence cannot be enhanced – nor can parents be protected as consumers – by subjecting them to inspection procedures which undermine them.

So what is it, Mr Maclure, about these 'procedures' which destroys professional 'competence and confidence'? The Handbook of Inspection which determines what inspectors do and how they behave has, remember, been warmly received by headteachers across the country. Perhaps 'procedures' is the wrong word. Perhaps what Maclure is really objecting to here is the fact that a report is published on the school's performance. I grant that some teachers and headteachers will find this worrying. But is Maclure, or anyone else, arguing that it is the wrong thing to do? That parents should be kept in the dark? The answer is, yes, some within the educational establishment do think this. Professor Brighouse, for example, the Chief Education Officer in Birmingham, argues that if a school fails its inspection it should be given time to improve. The problem, he believes, should be kept in the educational family, and parents told only what it is good for them to hear. I can only say (and I write here as a parent rather than as the ex-Chief Inspector) that I find his condescension appalling. As a parent, I have a right to know what is going on. If the school my child attends fails its inspection I want to be told – now. But then, Brighouse and, I suspect, Maclure, do not really approve of inspection at all. It is the very fact, perhaps, that teachers are accountable that, in Maclure's view, demoralises them.

'Such matters', he writes, 'will doubtless be attended to over time, as the education system as a whole domesticates OFSTED and its ways are tempered by day-to-day realities'. The sadness is that he is probably right. OFSTED will be, in his chilling and revealing word, 'domesticated'. 'Professional inspectorates', as the Citizens' Charter warned us, 'can easily become part of a closed professional world'. The establishment will win. Not because there is any evidence to support the views of Maclure and other pundits. It will win because so many of the educational great and the good have had so much to say against OFSTED, because the whole debate has become politicised, because the liberal press falls over itself to give maximum publicity to each and every attack, and because politicians, many of whom, like Estelle Morris, are ex-teachers, do not have the stomach for the fight.

It is sad because the 'competence and confidence' of good teachers is enhanced by inspection. Good teachers know that they have nothing to fear from OFSTED. They know, too, that colleagues who cannot teach effectively make their own lives more difficult. Twenty-five years on, I can remember sitting in a staffroom complaining that I had had to spend the first ten minutes of a lesson getting the children down off the wall because they had been allowed to run riot by the teacher who had, using the word loosely, taught them the previous lesson. One lazy and incompetent teacher can damage the reputation of dozens of other teachers. More generally, it is, or ought to be, obvious, as I said earlier, that the better teachers teach, the more children will learn. The more children learn, the more positive the image of the teaching profession in the eyes of the general public. And the more positive this image the higher morale will be in the profession. Maclure cannot see it, but, in identifying both excellent and weak practice, celebrating the former and speaking out against the latter, inspection contributes to a virtuous circle that does more to restore the self-confidence of the teaching profession than any number of government advertising campaigns designed to remind the public that nobody forgets a good teacher.

Finally, the most interesting question of all: Has OFSTED a future? Indeed, should OFSTED have a future? Has the time come to listen to the unions and the academics and many within the teaching profession and abandon school inspection? Schools could then evaluate their own performance. Local education authorities could 'moderate', whatever this might mean, the rigour of their scrutiny procedures and some sort of report would, presumably, be published. What would be lost if Estelle Morris were to take this radical step?

The answer is everything and nothing. Everything if OFSTED were to continue the struggle to preserve its independence, to speak out on behalf of parents, and to cut through the vested interests – academic, bureaucratic and professional – that have undermined standards and driven so many good teachers from the profession. Nothing if, in these new conciliatory times, the independence of the organisation is to be sacrificed on the altar of partnership as inspectors compete one with another to cosy up to ministers and their officials and to re-engineer themselves as the teacher's friend. If it is to be the latter, OFSTED should be abolished tomorrow and its multi-million pound budget used to fund an extra few thousand classroom assistants or pay young teachers a salary upon which they can afford to live.

In that my temporary successor, Mike Tomlinson, is about to retire and a new appointment has just been announced, the jury is, I suppose, out. I have to say, though, that the omens are not good. Last autumn, OFSTED launched a consultation on the future of inspection. Mr Tomlinson said: 'I want an inspection system to be something we do with schools rather than to schools. The inspection process is one that should be done with the school playing an active part rather than being a passive recipient'. He would not have said this without ministerial approval. All, it seems, will be OK if the adults consent, particularly if the experience is mutually enjoyable. He added, hoping, I suppose, to persuade himself if nobody else, that he was 'quite convinced that none of the proposals will affect the rigour and objectivity of inspection'.

He would hardly admit to anxieties, would he? Will his successor be able to deliver, however? Is it possible to reconcile what are mutually exclusive objectives? Of course it is not. A system of school inspection that is 'more responsive to the different circumstances and priorities of schools and the policies of government' and 'more supportive of school improvement' is unlikely to be a rigorous system. What after all do weasel words like 'responsive' mean? That schools in (to use the jargon) 'challenging circumstances' need to be approached more sympathetically than those that are located in leafy suburbs? If it does, it is a dangerously retrograde step. We want realism, yes, as to the challenge the school faces, but the expectations must be common: all schools must be assessed on a common template. If they are not, then it is the disadvantaged children who need education the most who will, once again, lose out. Why, moreover, should inspection respond to the particular 'priorities' a school might have, or, indeed, to the policies of government? It is what, no doubt, schools and politicians want, but it is a move away from the ideal of an inspection as a mirror that shows the school how well it is performing, warts and all. And 'supportive of improvement'? Well, the words may mean nothing. Inspection has always been supportive of improvement in the sense that the identification of a weakness is the first and necessary step towards its eradication. If, though, the implication is that in future inspectors are to gush over the positive and turn discretely away from the negative, then this is not, I am afraid, a major step forward.

These are, in fact, real cake and eat it proposals. Rigour is to be maintained, but teachers are no longer to be graded. Schools, as a first step, no doubt, towards a system in which they review their own performance, are to be able to 'select one issue for inspection based on their own self-evaluation'. The short inspection, which was previously given to the most successful schools, is now, despite the fact that 25 per cent of eleven-year-olds are still not being taught to read, to be the norm for all primary schools. The inspection is to be 'matched' to 'relevant school and national issues' whilst simultaneously offering 'a balanced assessment of each school and the education service as a whole'. It is a confusion which suggests, in its typical New Labour desire to be all things to all people, a disturbing degree of ministerial influence over what is meant to be an independent body. The choice is crystal clear. Ms Morris cannot have it both ways and neither can OFSTED. On the one hand, a domesticated inspectorate that has been brought back into the education establishment and integrated once more into the political machine. On the other, an Inspectorate that seeks on behalf of parents and their children to challenge the progressive consensus that continues to dominate the world of education. Which is it to be? My money, sadly, is on the former.

CHAPTER 5

Local Education Authorities

The priority, Tony Blair told us, in the run up to the last election, was to be reform of the public services. Waste and bureaucracy were, it seemed, about to be cut. The private sector would be brought in to help tackle the problems that had festered for so long. Headteachers were to be freed from the shackles of external regulation. Predictably enough, Mr Blair's words provoked a great deal of hostile reaction. The public sector unions sprang to the defence of their employees. The Local Government Association argued, yet again, that local education authorities were essential to the crusade to raise standards. At the time of writing (October 2001), things have gone very quiet. It is impossible to say whether the Government is genuinely committed to reform or whether Mr Blair's rhetoric, like most pre-election flannel, will simply wither in the delivery.

Looking back, it has to be said that the story thus far on the reform of LEAs is not encouraging. Successive governments have challenged the LEA hegemony and successive governments have failed. The debate about the role of local government has dragged on for the best part of twenty years, and LEAs continue to function much as they always did. Indeed, if Christine Whatford, Director of Education in Hammersmith and Fulham, is to be believed, supporters of LEAs should celebrate decisions taken in the last Parliament. 'At last', she wrote in an article published in the *Times Educational Supplement*, 'the question mark over the future of LEAs has been removed'. She continued: 'What matters is that schools and LEAs have enough money to do what they need to do and that schools aren't overburdened with things they would rather not do themselves'. Congratulations, Christine. I have rarely read a sentence that begs so many questions. What do LEAs 'need' to do? What are these 'things' that schools would rather not do themselves? Does Christine Whatford, or anyone else for that matter, really believe that there is a consensus amongst headteachers as to what responsibilities they do or do not want to assume? There is not. There is neither a political nor an educational consensus. Faced with significant internal opposition to reform, the last Labour government cobbled together a compromise that had little intellectual credibility and is unlikely to survive deepening headteacher scepticism. If the Prime Minister really wants things to be done differently, then, whatever the lack of progress thus far, the necessary changes could be achieved.

The Government would, of course, like you to think that a great deal has already been done. In January 2001 the DFEE as it then was reported that twenty LEAs had either contracted out their back-office functions or were in the process of so doing. In addition, of course, from April 2001 the expectation is that LEAs will devolve at least 85 per cent of their funding to schools – a move that, in theory at any rate, ought to strengthen school autonomy and reduce the power of the LEA.

A recent report from the city analysts Capital Strategies judges that the 'outsourcing sector will grow rapidly over the next five years' and that 'outsourcing specialists appear to be responding to the opportunities'. Things must be changing, mustn't they, if big business is enthusiastically spotting new market possibilities? And a government that in February 2001 announced a £1.8 million project aimed at 'encouraging LEAs to develop innovative ways of working with the private sector and other partner organisations' shouldn't be criticised, surely, for failing to move the agenda on?

The answer is that it should. Things did not in any significant sense change during the course of the last Parliament. The reason in part was that the DFEE and Number 10 did not see eye to eye on the future of LEAs. The DFEE tended, as always, to be protective of the status quo. Why, I could never quite decide. In part, the answer is that there was a lingering political commitment to local government. The rhetoric, of course, celebrated a non-ideological pragmatism, but the reality was different. Not every New Labour leopard found it that easy to change his or her political spots, and some at least of those who had once upon a time played a big role in local government struggled unsuccessfully to free themselves from the shackles of town hall municipalism. Officials felt a perhaps inevitable solidarity with their town hall brothers. A bureaucrat is a bureaucrat: the mind set is fundamentally similar whatever the political context. Whitehall or Town Hall, it does not matter. Both know best, or better anyway than individual schools. And then there is the natural, institutional tendency of the DFEE/DfES to defend the existing state of affairs, whatever it might be, the innate conservatism (with, of course, a small 'c') of the civil service, the scepticism which invariably meets radical ideas, be they from the left or the right.

The Number 10 view was, initially at least, radical. The feeling was that too many LEAs were failing to deliver. The decision was taken to speed up the programme of OFSTED LEA inspections so that every LEA could be inspected before the election.

Number 10 wanted the widest possible evidence base upon which to draw in formulating new reforms of local government. The Prime Minister was determined to know the extent of the failure, and was, I thought at the time, fully prepared to use the new legislation and privatise each and every LEA function that OFSTED found wanting.

In the event, of course, it has not turned out like this. Huge sums of public money have been wasted employing consultants to second guess OFSTED's judgements and/or to draw up what have often been indefensibly complex contracts. Ministerial decisions have been delayed for month after month. And, not surprisingly, many in the private sector have become increasingly disillusioned – by the process and, more fundamentally, by what after all the waiting has turned out to be a decision to do as little as possible in order to avoid upsetting councillors and local Labour MPs. The more limited the scope of the outsourcing, the less likely it is that there will be worthwhile change, and the less the enthusiasm of the contractor who really wants to make a difference.

Who knows? This second Blair administration may yet turn out to have a new, more courageous approach. Ministers might conceivably be more willing, in the interests of the fabled standards agenda, to rock a few boats, but somehow I doubt it. Everything depends upon the Prime Minister's determination and Estelle Morris's willingness to listen and ability to deliver. Few who know what happened in the last Parliament will be holding their breath.

The test case for me was Leeds. The OFSTED report was damning. The Authority went into complete denial, accused OFSTED of political bias, and refused to accept that any of the criticisms had any validity whatsoever. There was, predictably, absolute opposition to any form of privatisation. After a great deal of toing and froing, and scrutiny, no doubt, within the privacy of the DFEE, of ministerial navels, the end result, to quote Capital Strategies, is that a company has been set up to run educational services in Leeds that is 'wholly owned' by the City Council. Capita is to provide advice. The existing education authority staff have been transferred to the new company. The board is to include two Capita and two council representatives. Given the catalogue of woe uncovered by OFSTED, I cannot believe that this attempt to appear to do something while desperately wanting to avoid upsetting anyone is going to deliver the improvements that are needed in Leeds.

Capital Strategies are right, however. The market is 'much wider than simply providing services to failing LEAs'. We will, I am sure, see significant further private sector involvement as LEAs respond to the spirit of the times, and, recognising that it is in their interests to move down this road, enter into 'partnerships' with different contractors. The question is whether these developments are likely to make any real difference. The further and crucial question is what kind of difference we want to make.

A cursory glance at the eleven projects that the DfES is currently supporting suggests that radical change is no longer on the agenda. The name of the game now is to do what is currently being done, but to do it, hopefully, with greater efficiency. This would be fine if the current approach to school support and school improvement was in principle the right one. It is not. We have, therefore, a situation in which public money is being used to prop up an inadequate, if not failed system. In that there are profits to be made, the private sector is unlikely to complain, and why should it? However the taxpayer, if he knew what was happening, might. Many headteachers without doubt will.

So much in these eleven projects is taken for granted. Havering LEA, for example, is exploring, with the support of the consultancy firm KPMG, 'the potential for federations/clusters of schools to deliver better procurement of goods and services, rationalisation of support services and programmes for raising standards'. Procurement from whom? The LEA, I presume, despite the fact that other providers might well be able to offer a better deal. The LEA's support services are to be 'rationalised', whatever this means, but nobody asks whether Havering really needs to deliver these services. Nobody questions whether the LEA should necessarily be providing 'programmes of school improvement'. Is it, moreover, 'programmes' that are wanted? Do not different schools have different needs? Would it not be better to pursue the ideal of flexibility, the ability to deliver an individualised response? None of these questions seems even to have been considered. The assumption is that the current approach is in essence right and that the only issue is how what is being done now can be done more efficiently.

The potential for unnecessary complication is, in several of these schemes, infinite. Indeed, the greater the complexity, it seems, the greater the appeal to the DfES. If I were a headteacher in North Somerset, I would certainly be asking myself whether we really needed to develop 'a model whereby a partnership (of North Somerset LEA, Capita, CEA, Rathbone CI, and local head-teachers' associations, governors, etc) is given responsibility for delivering and securing LEA services'. Eh? Does this mean that North Somerset is going to continue to deliver services or not? And if it isn't, then who is? Given the encyclopaedic list of partners, what does the ominous 'etc' signify? How much is this partnership going to cost? And, the $64,000 question, why is an LEA as small as North Somerset contemplating an approach of such Byzantine complexity that it is inevitably going to distract headteachers from their core task of raising standards in their schools?

Some of these initiatives inspire, of course, more confidence than others. If we want our LEAs to be more efficient, and, if they are to continue to exist, we obviously do, then it might well be a good idea for Tower Hamlets LEA to become an 'operational unit' of the outsourcing company Serco. But, once again, there are questions to be asked: What is it going to cost? Would this money be better spent on other things? Would it be better to give it to headteachers to spend in their schools? And, more fundamentally, are we sure that everything that is currently done by Tower Hamlets for, with and to its schools needs to be done? What scope in this exercise is there for a radical rethink?

The comments David Blunkett made on these initiatives when he was Secretary of State reveal the leap that is now needed if the Prime Minister's aspirations are to be realised. 'Our investment', he said, 'in these local projects will provide ideas and real examples of delivering education services to many other local authorities across the country'. Well, I suppose he may just be right, but the presumption is clear. LEAs will continue to have some kind of responsibility, albeit in 'partnership' (that wonderful, ubiquitous buzz word) with the private sector and others, for the delivery of services. The possibility that the LEA might have no legitimate role is not even contemplated. He continued: 'I believe it is important for schools to be self-managed and for headteachers to have the flexibility to improve education at a [sic] school level. Over the last four years, they have had increased financial autonomy'.

Excuse me? Wasn't this the government that invented seventy-odd categories for the Standards Fund and earmarked everything that moved? The government that abolished grant maintained schools, and, whatever it might have thought it was doing, opened the door to greater LEA interference in the running of successful schools? Yes, Mr Blunkett attempted towards the end of his time as Secretary of State for Education to make political capital out of the fact that prescription is, apparently, to be reduced. But he himself was, of course, responsible for the torrent of regulation in the first place. Born again he may be, but I am not yet persuaded that our previous Secretary of State was, shall I say, a genuine apostle of school autonomy. What, moreover, are the 'flexibilities' that head-teachers need if they are to improve their schools? Should they have to bid for money and subordinate their own priorities to those of the DfES or the LEA? Should they have the flexibility (assuming that more of the available resource is eventually devolved to them) to buy whatever support they want from whomsoever they want?

Blunkett then played the failing school card: 'Nevertheless weak schools cannot be left to succeed or fail alone. There are also some essential functions more sensibly carried out through the local authority or centrally'. Of course, weak schools cannot be left to fail, but this obvious truth is no argument for the retention of the whole unsatisfactory status quo. Are we, moreover, sure that we know which functions should be carried out centrally? What does 'centrally' mean? Is it the LEA? Is it Whitehall? Is it some form of regional government? In a rational world we would by now have answers to these questions, and, until we do, the huge potential of the private sector to support teachers in raising standards will never be realised.

Ms Morris has a choice. She can either travel still further down the road of centralised state control or she can act upon her predecessor's belated recognition that schools should have the freedom to determine their own destiny.

For obvious reasons, ministers have been reluctant to come clean about why they believe that state control is the answer. The truth is they think that standards in too many schools are too bloody low and that, left to its own devices, the teaching profession will never deliver the improvements the electorate wants (which means that they might not win the next election).

The only way forward is for everyone to march in step behind the Standards and Effectiveness Unit. Schools must be persuaded (forced? cajoled? bribed?) to participate in initiatives that will (the officials hope) transform teaching.

If this is to be the approach, then LEAs, aided and abetted no doubt by the private sector, have a future. It is not a very glorious future, but there you are: it is something. They will function as an outpost of the DfES. Their officials will in effect be Ms Morris's foot soldiers. To an extent they already are, but it could well become much worse (or better, depending upon your point of view).

I can see the temptation. The National Literacy and Numeracy Strategies have been a significant success. I nevertheless believe that it is a temptation that must be resisted. First, because, while the pedagogy encouraged by the NLS and NNS is essentially sensible, there is no guarantee that this will be the case in future initiatives. I simply do not trust officials in the Standards and Effectiveness Unit to promote the right ideas and we all know that Secretaries of State can be a tad gullible when it comes to duff advice. Indeed, the Key Stage 3 initiative suggests that we should hone our scepticism of politicians and officials alike. Then, second, my experience in education over the last thirty years leads me to believe that there is a very close link between autonomy and effectiveness: the greater the professional freedom, the higher the teacher's satisfaction; the higher that satisfaction and self-esteem, the more likely it is that standards of pupil achievement will rise.

This is not to suggest that we should return to the laissez-faire days of the sixties and seventies. Accountability is essential and intervention vital if performance is poor. But intervention ought to be in inverse proportion to success: this second Labour Government must dust down the mantra that was meant to guide the actions of the first.

It is, or ought to be, very simple. Define (and raise, through a reform of the public examination system) expectations of what children should know at different stages in their school careers. Devolve responsibility for delivery to the individual school. Ensure that the school has the resources it needs, and, what is equally if not more important, the freedom to determine what needs doing when. Hold the governing body and the head-teacher responsible for the school's performance. Intervene when necessary.

Where does the LEA fit into this model of school improvement? It does not. There is no need for an LEA to monitor what is happening in its schools. OFSTED will inspect regularly, evaluate the test and examination results (and all the other data that is now available) and bring forward the next inspection if problems seem to be emerging. LEAs pretend that regular school visiting by their advisers is crucial if they are to keep their finger on the pulse, but this is just that: a pretence, and a pretty patronising pretence at that.

Neither is there necessarily any support role. This idea of 'support' is one of the great contemporary education myths. It is in everybody's interests to keep it going. Teachers, backed by their unions, can argue that all would be well if only they had more 'support'. LEAs like the idea for the obvious reason that it generates a lot of work for people who otherwise would have nothing to do. The DfES and its quangos believe that the more 'advice' they publish and supportive initiatives they fund, the quicker standards will rise. They would, wouldn't they?

There are three problems. The first is that most of the documents that flood into schools rapidly gather dust and most of the initiatives have little long-term impact. Support does not work when it is dumped from above. Second, it costs. The more ambitious the local and national government programme of support, the less money there is for schools. And, third, the support industry sustains a culture of dependency and deference: the belief that somewhere, someone has the answer and that all our problems would be solved if only we could tap into his wisdom. In fact, as anyone who has tried to change anything knows, it is not like this. New ideas can make a difference. On occasion, they are vital. But in the end what matters is the graft: the determination and self-belief of those who work within the school to tackle the problem. A government, aided and abetted by LEAs that know what they must say and do if they are to survive, that prides itself on the level of support it is giving to schools is, in fact, contributing to the problem. It is wasting money that could otherwise be used to much better effect in schools and it is undermining the can-do self-confidence upon which all improvements depend.

There remains the issue of the school that has no confidence, the school that cannot manage its own destiny. Mr Blunkett was right. Someone has to intervene. Support in these circumstances is certainly needed. But is it the LEA that should be giving that support? The answer is no. If the LEA can deliver better support than other providers, including, of course, private sector companies, then that is fine. But there is no rational justification for the present monopoly situation. If, moreover, we look at the evidence, we have to ask whether LEAs are the best agency to support failing schools.

By and large, when a school has failed its inspection, the LEA support has been adequate. Far too many schools designated as having serious weaknesses are, however, failing their next inspection, having had, it seems, little or no support from their LEA. The monopoly must be challenged. David Blunkett's statement that failing schools cannot be left to fail is an argument not so much for the retention of the LEA as an acknowledgement that this is one of the areas in which private sector involvement is most needed.

Ms Morris would do well to reflect on her experience as a minister. She should acknowledge the emptiness of the outsourcing rhetoric and the shoddiness of the compromises that were made. She should question the complexity of the procurement processes. She should accept that public money has been wasted on private sector consultancies that were not needed, and, more fundamentally, that, because nobody has really been prepared to challenge the status quo, the private sector is currently being used to sustain a situation which, sooner or later, will implode. She should call for the proverbial blank sheet and muster her political courage.

The power of the various vested interests might make change difficult in practice, but the principles ought not to be hard to establish.

There is, on the one hand, the individual school, and, on the other, there is the DfES. The school most people (in theory, at least) now think should be self-managing. The DfES's powers, for the reasons I have outlined above, ought to be curtailed. Ms Morris should abolish the Standards and Effectiveness Unit (SEU) and end the flow of regulation and the frenzy of initiative. The resource currently consumed by the civil servants should be devolved to teachers in their classrooms. If they are really needed, the management of new initiatives can always be contracted out. The education charity, The Centre for British Teachers (CFBT) manages, after all, the National Literacy and Numeracy Strategies.

Where does this leave the LEA? The DfES will be doing less and will not, therefore, need its foot soldiers. Self-managing schools will be just that: they will have the money and they will decide which services they need and from whom they want to buy them. This may or may not be the LEA. What Ms Morris ought to encourage is a genuine market. We have such a market in inspection. Why not in the provision of services to schools?

I can hear the reaction of officials and elected members as I write. We already have such a market, they will retort. We do not. We have LEAs that have 'offered' schools various kinds of contracts under which they buy back services, but the current situation is a very long way from an open market. They will suggest that schools have neither the time nor the inclination to identify the provider that is best for them. I can only say that I find this a deeply patronising suggestion.

Some (mainly primary) headteachers do worry, of course, about their administrative burdens and are fearful of new responsibilities. I sympathise. I have always argued that the headteacher's core task is that of educational leadership. There is an important distinction to be made here, however: headteachers, primary as well as secondary, should be able to decide for themselves what is best for their schools, they should not have to deal with the details of the administration that the decision brings. If more money is devolved to schools, headteachers will have the chance to purchase, if that is what they want to do, more administrative support. They might decide to pay their secretary more to reward her for extra responsibility or to buy extra hours. Whatever, the point is that there is no need to fear the responsibility if support is available to deal with the administration.

The suggestion was made when I was Chief Inspector that if the government were to go down this road, the DfES would have to regulate the market. It would not. The Government allows the headteacher as a private citizen to decide which car best suits his or her particular needs. It has no problem with an open market in text books. Why then assume that headteachers cannot decide for themselves who they want to employ as a consultant?

The role, then, of the private sector in providing services to schools ought to be just that: it should provide. It should not, remember Mr Blunkett's eleven projects, be drawn into convoluted schemes which are intended to prop up the existing flawed system and which are likely to make life more, not less difficult for headteachers. It will be accountable, moreover, in the market place. There is no need for any kind of bureaucratic regulation, national or local.

There is one further point to make about the provision of services to schools. Some services are difficult for individual schools to manage on their own. Most headteachers say, for example, that they do not want to have anything to do with school transport. We should respect this view, but we should not jump to the conclusion that this is an argument for retaining the LEA. The organisation of school transport is a purely technical job that could and should be done by other units within the Council – or, indeed, by a private sector company.

But LEAs do not simply provide services to schools. They have, it is argued, a strategic function. They run a variety of services that are nowadays grouped under the banner of lifelong learning. And, what is the most interesting argument of all for their continuing existence, their elected members decide upon issues that transcend the interests of individual schools and which have a genuine democratic significance. Let us take each of these points in turn.

It is hard, given the extent to which, for better or worse, the DfES controls the educational agenda, to give much credence to the view that a strategic overview by the local authority adds very much. The National Curriculum is the National Curriculum, the National Literacy Strategy the National Literacy Strategy. The notion of such an overview raises some interesting questions about the extent to which schools do and should manage their own affairs. Time and time again, I have asked LEA officials and members the simple question: 'Where does strategic leadership end and local management begin?' I have never received a satisfactory answer. Neither has anyone ever responded very convincingly to my even simpler follow up: 'What do you mean by strategic leadership?'

What 'leadership' do headteachers need? Is this not yet another patronising bureaucratic assumption? Michael Barber's argument when he worked in education that standards will only rise if the Prime Minister is personally at the helm has always made me cringe. I will never forget the documentation Tim Brighouse supplied us when OFSTED inspected Birmingham LEA. It was not the bulk, the grandiose ambition of the many different initiatives, the unintelligibility of much of the prose. It was the statement in black and white that no school, however effective, could remain successful without the support of its local authority. I have no idea whether Brighouse still believes this, but, sadly, I suspect he does. It says it all.

Our two professors will no doubt reply that I simply do not understand what New Labour means by 'strategic management'. I do, actually, and I am not convinced. The thinking comes from America. We have moved, they want us to believe, beyond the 'old dichotomous view' that 'local is good, central is bad or visa versa'. I am quoting from a paper published by The Center for Educational Outreach and Innovation at Columbia University entitled *Re-Centralization or Strategic Management?* that has clearly influenced Barber and therefore Blunkett. The argument is that 'top managers' (Barber and Brighouse) and 'local educators' (headteachers) each have 'a unique and important contribution' to make. The 'former holds the big picture, the benchmarks across settings, access to external resources, and the authority to intervene when things go wrong'. Familiar? 'Meanwhile, the delivery units (schools and classrooms) – having the close-up picture and the best knowledge of students and families in their schools – are free to determine means and proximate ends, leaving final, summative assessment to those at the top of the system'. Don't ask me what a 'proximate' end might be, but thanks any way for the freedom. And thanks, too, for the relationship you are offering. 'The top and the bottom of the organisation', we are told will relate one to another in a 'synergistic, dynamic, and self-reinforcing way'. Now you know. No wonder headteacher morale is rising by the minute. No wonder I am sceptical about strategic management.

Then there is the argument that the drive to raise standards in schools is only one aspect of the Council's strategic responsibilities? 'Joint action', Ms Whatford writes in the article I quoted from earlier, 'between education, housing, and social services committees and through partnership [that word again] with external agencies such as the NHS, the police and the voluntary and private sectors' is the answer if initiatives like the Neighbourhood Renewal Strategy are to be delivered.

I agree, but what are we talking about here? The invention of new, multi-disciplinary initiatives which will, it is hoped, solve the problem of social exclusion? If this is the game, and of course it is, then I want nothing to do with it. It will generate yet more hot air in committee rooms and waste yet more public money. What we need is better management: a remorseless attention at every level in the system to the day-to-day detail of service delivery and much better co-ordination of service delivery when different agencies or organisations are involved. At present, as all too many headteachers will tell you, the co-ordination is non-existent. If LEAs spent less time brooding on their strategic responsibilities and focused on the delivery of the services for which they are currently responsible, life would be a great deal easier for a lot of headteachers.

But LEAs do not need to manage anything. They no more need to manage the Youth Service than they did the Careers Service. The argument that every service impacts (or ought to impact) upon every other and that the LEA has, therefore, to do

everything is a complete red herring. If co-ordination is important, as it obviously is, then the need to co-ordinate can be built
into the contracts that are let.

What, though, of the suggestion that LEAs must be retained
in the interests of local democracy? I believe that schools can
and should decide what services they want to buy from whom
and that there is no need for any 'accountability' other than
that of the market place. These services (property, personnel,
educational advice, and so on) are technical, professional
matters. They have no democratic significance. Some issues,
however, in the management and administration of education
involve more than one school and some have genuine political
implications. I am thinking of the deep controversy that always
surrounds a proposal to shut a school or reorganise education
in a particular area; conflicts over admissions when a parent
cannot secure a place for his child in an over-subscribed school;
and the provision of extra resources for children with special
educational needs. Such issues involve the rights of individual
citizens. They are not simply technical.

Do they mean that the LEA has in some form to be retained?
Not necessarily. The rights and wrongs of admissions and special
needs support are ultimately a matter for the Ombudsman and
many headteachers (certainly with regard to admissions and
exclusions) do not exactly think that their LEAs add much
value. LEAs do not, moreover, have a particularly good track
record when it comes to ensuring that empty places are taken
out of the system. These, admittedly difficult, decisions might
well be better taken by regional offices of the DfES, and if they
were, it would not, I believe, make very much difference to the
democratic rights of local citizens.

Finally, there is the argument advanced by defenders of the
LEA faith that privatisation is wrong in principle because it under-
mines local control. This is nonsense. Take school transport. I

know of no LEA that believes that it must own every bus and employ every driver. What happens, of course, is that the LEA determines the need that has to be met, draws up a contract, decides upon the best contractor, and then monitors the delivery of the contract. If the contractor is not providing an adequate service, then the LEA, acting for the local communities it represents, can intervene. And this is exactly what would happen if in future outsourcing were to become the norm. The Council would still be in charge. Local people would not in any sense be disenfranchised.

Note that I use the term 'council'. I do not think that we need LEAs in their present form to monitor contracts. A small group of appropriately trained officials in the Chief Executive's office, reporting to an equally small group of councillors could do the job more efficiently. There will not after all be many contracts that will need to be managed by the LEA as opposed to the school and the driving imperative has to be the elimination of unnecessary bureaucracy.

As yet, there has been little or no discussion as to how these local accountabilities might best be discharged. This debate is needed, and needed urgently. The danger is that, in the absence of any hard thought about accountability and the role of the LEA, we rush yet further down the road that was travelled in the last Parliament. The Government will try to be all things to all men, to placate every vested interest, and will end up achieving very little. That would be a disaster for Estelle Morris, for Mr Blair, and above all for schools.

CHAPTER 6

Universities

I

I should not, I know. It is not fair. The temptation, however, is too great to resist. Here is John Henry Newman's eloquent defence of education as an enterprise that cannot and must not be reduced to any utilitarian end:

> Such knowledge is not a mere extrinsic or accidental advantage, which is ours today and another's tomorrow, which may be got up from a book, and easily forgotten again, which we can command or communicate at our pleasure, which we can borrow for the occasion, carry about in our head, and take into the market; it is an acquired illumination, it is a habit, a personal possession, and an inward endowment. And this is the reason, why it is more correct, as well as more usual, to speak of a University as a place of education, than of instruction, though, when knowledge is concerned, instruction would at first sight have seemed the more appropriate word. We

are instructed, for instance, in manual exercises, in the fine and useful arts, in trades, and in ways of business; for these are methods, which have little or no effect upon the mind itself, are contained in rules committed to memory, tradition, use, and bear upon an end external to themselves. But Education is a higher word; it implies an action upon our mental nature, and the formation of a character; it is something individual and permanent, and is commonly spoken of in connexion with religion and virtue. When then we speak of the communication of Knowledge as being Education, we thereby really imply that Knowledge is a state or condition of mind; and since cultivation of mind is surely worth seeking for its own sake, we are thus brought once more to the conclusion, which the word 'Liberal' and the word 'Philosophy' have already suggested, that there is a Knowledge, which is desirable, though nothing comes of it, as being of itself a treasure, and a sufficient remuneration of years of labour . . .

And here is Margaret Hodge, Minister for Lifelong Learning and Higher Education and mistress, it seems, of the utilitarian end. She is upset because Graham Zellick, the Vice Chancellor of the University of London, had the temerity to suggest that the Government's ambitious proposal to extend participation in higher education to 50 per cent of young people under thirty was 'mindless and misguided'.

'What nonsense', Ms Hodge wrote in an article published in the *Guardian*. 'In the sixties when he [Zellick] and I went to university we were part of a privileged elite . . . In those days 50 per cent would have been seen as a social dream. Today, however, it is an economic necessity . . . if we want to tackle our productivity agenda and work to maintain and enhance our competitiveness . . . Having said that, of course, we also have ambitions to build a more equal and inclusive society . . . It is a shocking fact that many children from lower socio-economic groups do not hear of higher education as an option for them during their years at school. Their opportunities will not be enhanced by elitist pronouncements from vice chancellors'.

So there. That has put this errant academic firmly in his place. Professor Zellick, Mr Hodge believes should, 'Stop whinging and help us get on with the job'. The trouble is that the job as she sees it is the destruction of the university as Newman conceived it. On the one hand, social inclusion and the 'productivity agenda', on the other the recognition that education is 'an acquired illumination, a habit, a personal possession, and an inward endowment'. The juxtaposition says it all, doesn't it?

I have sunk, having written that sentence, into a deep gloom. What is the point? What is the point in my writing this book or, for that matter, anyone writing or saying anything? Every time the Prime Minister or the Chancellor or Estelle Morris open their mouths to talk about education they tell us that it is important because it contributes to our economic and social good. This is a Prime Minister who, before he realised that it might not be playing too well in the press, was only too keen to commend the virtues of Cool Britannia, who is openly dismissive of history and tradition, who is desperate to modernize everything that moves. The university as a place where, to quote the philosopher Michael Oakeshott, a student has 'the opportunity of education in conversation with his teachers, his fellows and himself, and where he is not encouraged to confuse education with training for a profession, with learning the tricks of the trade', is a prime target for his transforming zeal. Newman and Oakeshott, in the unlikely event that he were ever to read them, are not going to change Mr Blair's mind. We do not even talk of universities any more. It is 'higher education' and 'lifelong learning', whatever the latter in practice might be. To question the Government's policies is to be dismissed as an elitist whinger. And, what is more disturbing still, the majority of vice chancellors seem only too happy to collude in the destruction of our universities. They moan, of course, about under funding and the level to which academic salaries have sunk, but they are happy enough to go along with the expansion of their empires. There is no point.

Defeatism will not, however, do. The issues are too important. If the Government pursues its policy of expansion the consequences will be dire: dire, for the thousands of students who will find themselves locked into three years of sub-degree study that is unlikely to bring any real intellectual satisfaction and may well not lead to worthwhile employment; dire, for those universities which are still places 'where a tradition of learning is preserved and extended'; dire for us all, in that the survival of a society that understands what it is to participate in civilized and humane conversation depends upon the preservation of universities that are worthy of the name.

Mr Blair and his Minister for Lifelong Learning cannot be allowed to pursue their profoundly destructive programme unchallenged. Graham Zellick's fellow vice-chancellors should follow his courageous lead. The leader writers and columnists should enter the fray and question the basic assumptions. It is time to ask the obvious questions that should have been asked back in 1997 when these policies started to emerge.

II

Let us begin with Ms Hodge's newspaper article. She tells us that:

Research suggests that a 10% increase in the proportion of workers with a degree-level qualification would boost our gross domestic product by 3.5%. Our competitors recognise the value of a highly skilled labour force. The US, Canada and Japan already have more people qualified to degree level than the UK. If we want to close the productivity gap we must close the skills gap, and that in part is about higher education. In the US, the proportion of the labour force with a degree is nearly 40% higher than in the UK. The labour market forecasts produced by the National Skills Task Force made another key point. They predicted that we would need a further 1.73m people with higher education skills to fill the new jobs which will emerge over the next decade. This constitutes 80% of the overall employment growth. We need to fill these new jobs in the knowledge economy with people with the right skills.

She does not tell us what research, and I do not know it. I do know that the Centre for Economic Performance recently published a report stating that 30 per cent of adults in Britain are over-educated. Somebody is 'over-educated' if they possess a higher level of qualification than is necessary for the job they are doing. 'The estate agent with a doctoral thesis will be no better at being an estate agent than someone with a degree; the graduate secretary will not need any of the skills acquired on a degree course to do the job properly'. It is true, of course, that large numbers of people are underqualified for the job they do (around 20 per cent according to some surveys), but the point here, as Ms Hodge admits but fails to understand, is that we need 'people with the right skills'. Her boss in the last parliament, David Blunkett, also drew upon research undertaken by the National Skills Task Force. He, however, noted that the highest level of skills shortages is in craft and skilled trades. These trades, he announced, need 120,000 new entrants a year. Talk to any Chamber of Commerce around the country and they will tell you that they cannot find them. The Construction Industry Training Board predicts that we will need 29,000 new plumbers and 35,000 new electricians over the next five years.

If your washing machine has sprung a leak recently, you will not need much convincing. The Government talks endlessly about the need for graduates in the Knowledge Economy, but the 'dirty little secret', remember, 'is the scarcity of the jobs that require more advanced skills'. We need plumbers and electricians, not, to take the letter C at random, graduates in Caribbean Studies, Caring Services, Childhood Studies, Chiropractice, Cinematics, Clothing Studies, Combined Studies, Communication Studies, Cosmetics, Contemporary Studies, Creative Therapies and Critical Theory.

Margaret Hodge is quite simply wrong. 'Promoting an ambitious increase in the number of young people in higher education' is not necessarily 'an economic imperative'. It could be a complete waste of everyone's time and money. Take the academic study of photography. She is no doubt aware that the photographic industry can absorb just 2 per cent of the students who complete a course in the subject. Two per cent! It is farcical. 'Teaching institutes', as Dunstan Pevera, the inventor of the Heliochrome photography printing process, stated recently, 'are turning out graduates like sausages, attempting to fill up shelves that are already full'. He continues: 'Most of these students are badly trained; they have no technical knowledge and are ill-equipped for the real world'. When he interviewed twenty-three applicants for a post of photography laboratory assistant, nobody knew who had invented photography. All had completed a diploma course. His conclusion? 'The present system is a waste of money and resources.'

He is right, it is, though Margaret Hodge, who wants to waste yet more money and resources, is unlikely to agree with me. Why does she assume that the recent economic success of the United States stems from the fact that a high percentage of the population are qualified to degree level? Can she demonstrate cause and effect? Of course she cannot. This, like so many of the assertions made so confidently day after day by ministers, is just that: an assertion. Does she not know that an undergraduate degree in the States is somewhat less rigorous and demanding than a degree (up until recently at least) in England? She is not comparing like with like. Neither does she seem to appreciate the fact that the economies of America and Japan are in a distinctly shaky state – hardly good examples to support her argument that the greater the number of graduates the more successful the economy.

Let us turn to the social justice argument. Ms Hodge suggests that Labour's aspiration to build 'a more equal and inclusive society' depends upon this expansion in student numbers. At present, the inequalities are, certainly, to use her word, 'startling'. Three out of every four young people from professional families go to university. One in ten working-class kids makes it. So much, as I have argued elsewhere in this book, for equality of opportunity. Those pundits and politicians who can, at the drop of a hat or sight of a microphone, work themselves up into a self-righteous fury at the prospect of selection or privatisation creating a 'two-tier' education system would do well to pause for a moment and reflect on what is a genuinely damning statistic. The egalitarian rhetoric has swept over us for years. We have dug ever deeper into our taxpayer's pocket. The politicians have tinkered endlessly with the legislation and the educational establishment has researched this and studied that and come up with one useless recommendation after another. All to no end. Margaret Hodge is in this, if no other, respect right. The children of the poor are not by definition more stupid than the children of the rich. More students from, to use the Higher Education Funding Council's discrete terminology, 'low participation neighbourhoods', ought to be studying at university. It is a scandal that they are not.

The Government's 50 per cent target is not, however, the answer. Forget for a moment the politics. Set aside the educational realities. Focus simply on the statistics. Mr Blair wants to increase the number of undergraduates by about 15 per cent. He thinks, presumably, that this expansion in numbers will crack the problem of working-class under-representation. But will it? The more likely outcome is that the new students will come from the professional classes that, on Ms Hodge's analysis, are already over represented. Ah, she will no doubt reply, but we have our Excellence Fellowship Awards which give teachers a 'placement' in a university. They will be so bowled over by the experience that they will return to their schools, fired with a missionary zeal, and persuade all the students who had decided that they were going to finish education and earn some money to change their minds and bang in an immediate application. If the issues were not so serious it would be comic. Let us, however, suspend disbelief and accept for the sake of argument that these new placements will transform the teacher's attitude. Let us concede that that teacher will inspire his students. We then have to face the fact that it is not ultimately a question of whether a young person wants to go to university. What matters is whether they have the intellectual ability and the knowledge to cope with and benefit from a university course. We have, to use Margaret Hodge's phrase, 'to raise attainment levels'. Unless, that is, we reduce our expectations and dumb down the courses. If the Government is determined, as Ms Hodge insists, to ensure that standards are maintained, 'placements' will do no more than scratch the surface of the problem. We still, remember, have a quarter of eleven-year-olds leaving primary school unable to read well enough to cope with the demands of the secondary school curriculum – and, as Margaret Hodge, MP for Barking and Dagenham, ought to know better than most, children from 'unskilled or working/manual backgrounds', are most certainly disproportionately represented in that group. She is whistling in the wind. We will never solve the problem of the under-representation in universities of young people from working-class backgrounds until we have solved the problem of failing schools. There is no other solution, whatever Ms Hodge might think and hope, no way in which the circle can be miraculously squared.

Politicians are not, however, known for their patience. They want their miracles and they want them while they are in office. Ms Hodge tells us that the Government would not dream of tinkering with the system in order to deliver demonstrable progress towards a more 'inclusive' society before, say, the next election. I wonder. There are three different ways in which tinkering is possible. Pressure can be exerted on the elite universities in order to persuade them to take more candidates from the wrong side of the tracks and, to make sure that the message is received, financial inducements can be offered and penalties threatened. New and different kinds of course can be introduced so as to make university study more 'attractive' to 'non-traditional' students – 'attractive', some would argue, being a euphemism for easier. And, the most obvious solution of all, universities can lower their expectations and admit students who are less knowledgeable and less intelligent than students are now, or, at least, once were. It is worth spending, despite Ms Hodge's protestations of innocence, a moment on each of these possibilities.

The pressure is obvious. The pusillanimous Labour Chairman of the Education Select Committee, Barry Shearman, chose to tiptoe very carefully around Gordon Brown's attack on Oxford University for failing to admit Laura Spence, a pupil from a Tyneside comprehensive school who was predicted to achieve five A grades at A level. But he, like everyone else outside the New Labour coterie, must have recognised that the Chancellor did not have a shred of evidence to support his ludicrous allegations. Brown's high-profile onslaught on 'elitism', privilege, the old-boy network and the rest of it had, however, its inevitable effect. Oxford, Cambridge and other universities are now very much on the defensive. The fact that they already do a great deal to attract applications from comprehensive school students is neither here nor there. They believe that the Government is out to get them.

Neither is it merely a war of words. The Prime Minister followed up his Chancellor's attack with an announcement that extra government money would be made available to encourage elite universities that do not admit sufficient numbers of young people from state schools in general and disadvantaged backgrounds in particular. It would have been nice if vice-chancellors had risen as a group and told the Government what it could do with these financial inducements. It is, after all, an extraordinary policy. The Prime Minister appears to believe that the future depends upon his ability to deliver 'a radical extension of opportunity'. In the run up to the last election, he addressed the nation. 'We are wasting too much of the talents of too many of the people', he said. 'The mission of any second term must be this: to break down the barriers that hold people back, to create upward mobility, a society that is open and genuinely based on merit and the equal worth of all'. It was a vision calculated to warm the egalitarian cockles of any floating voter's heart. But, hang on, what, having won the election, does he do? He loads the dice in favour of those who happen to have been born in the wrong part of town.

Francis Beckett's argument that 'the rich', who can 'buy for their children an education that places them on the fast track to power, wealth and influence', have had it their way for too long, cuts no ice whatsoever. Cannot Mr Blair see that the prize has to be awarded on merit if it is to be worth having? I agree that the figures Beckett quotes are extremely disturbing. 'The top five universities', he tells us, 'are Cambridge, Imperial College London, Oxford, London School of Economics and University College London. These universities accept about 9,600 new undergraduates each year, and almost half of them come from the 7 per cent of the population who attend fee-paying schools. The half of the population that comes from less affluent social classes contributes just 980 of the new undergraduates at these universities, or just over one in five'. But the conclusion is, or ought to be, obvious. We must raise the standards of state schools and, as I argue in the next chapter, we must find ways to make it possible for children from poor backgrounds to attend independent schools. To try to engineer the admission of young people who, albeit for no fault of their own, do not deserve their place at an elite university is in the long run to destroy the university. Admission has to be on merit and only on merit.

The most obvious example of new courses being introduced to cater for less qualified students is David Blunkett's much hyped invention: the two-year foundation degree. This new degree, which is intended to meet intermediate skill shortages, will, the Government hopes, make a major contribution to the increase in student numbers it needs if it is to deliver the Prime Minister's vision. There will be a mix of academic and work-place study and the intention is to focus on subjects such as hospitality, new media design and community enterprise. Newman would not approve, and neither does Baroness Perry, President of Lucy Cavendish College, Cambridge. 'The intro-duction of yet another qualification is', she thinks, 'unnecessary and unfortunate'. We already have HNDs, HNCs, Vocational A levels and Vocational GCSEs. Why invent a new degree that will inevitably cover similar ground to these existing qualifications and is likely to confuse employers and students? It is an obvious question to which there is an obvious answer. The Prime Minister wants more young people to have degrees. A traditional degree in, for example, History is unlikely to appeal, and, in any case, has no obvious contribution to make to our global competitiveness. We need, therefore, a new degree. The overlap, the potential for confusion: forget it, the priority is the political commitment to social inclusion. As the architect of the new degree, David Robertson, Professor of Public Policy at Liverpool Moores University puts it: 'If you want an inclusive higher education system you have to broaden its student base'. Indeed, you do. Tautological the proposition might be, but the truth is undeniable.

Foundation degrees may prove to be a good thing. They may turn out to be academically as demanding as any traditional degree. They may reach skill shortages other qualifications have not begun to touch. I am prepared to travel hopefully, but the rationale for their introduction does, on the face of it, look distinctly shaky. I accept, of course, that they are not intended to achieve the same standard as an honours degree, but they are still to be called 'degrees'. How, we might ask, can they be when the course lasts only two years as opposed to three, does not involve extra teaching, and is designed for students who would not be able to cope with the demands of a traditional degree? It is obvious. These are not degrees in the traditional sense of the word. What we have here is an exercise in branding. Ministers want more students in higher education. The word 'degree' has the right connotations. They decide, therefore, to call the course a degree. Whether or not it really is does not matter. In just the same way the General National Vocational Qualification has been re-labelled a Vocational A level. Does it matter? It does. Vocational courses ought to have their own integrity. To call them degrees is to invite the vacuous theoretical convolution we have seen so often in the past. It is, moreover, to devalue the existing academic currency. Courses ought to be distinct one from another, meeting different student needs, and serving different ends. They grow, it seems, less distinct by the day.

Neither is the problem simply the introduction of the foundation degree. There are now vast numbers of hitherto unheard of 'traditional' three-year degrees. I cited earlier some examples that began with the letter C. Move down the alphabet and interesting examples multiply. Golf Green Keeping? Horse Studies? Model Making? Packaging? Popular Music Studies? World Studies? Such courses may lead to interesting, well-paid jobs. They may contribute to our competitiveness in the global economy. They do not, however, constitute academic disciplines in any serious sense of the term. An academic discipline, to quote Anthony O'Hear, Professor of Philosophy at Bradford University, is 'a self-standing study with its own tradition and canon, with cognitive breadth and depth, and with high levels of analysis, synthesis and critical evaluation of intellectually demanding and significant material'. Popular Music Studies is not, on this, or, for that matter, any other definition, an academic discipline.

Professor Di Bentley, Director of the Schools of Education at Sheffield Hallam University, disagrees:

The Higher Education Funding Council have [sic] done a lot of work . . . in looking at what 'graduateness' may mean, whatever the content area of the degree. There has for a considerable number of years been an attempt to bring all universities to a common standard. It is also progressive, looking at what kinds of thing people are able to do at the end of their first, second and third years to try to have a hallmark for graduates. For example, there is an expectation that a graduate will have a high level of communication skills, be a high level problem solver and be able to critically analyse work. It does not matter what the content of the degree is if these standards are met . . . If your degree is in basketball what you have to ask is can you teach critical analysis, can you teach team working, and of course you can. If you can teach those things, and what's more it leads to employment, then what's wrong?

In my opinion, a great deal. The content of a degree, Professor Bentley argues, is irrelevant. All universities, she thinks, can be brought to a common standard. What matters is 'graduateness': the ability to communicate, solve problems, work in a team, and so on. What matters depends, of course, on our concept of a university. If, like Tony Blair and Gordon Brown, we judge the worth of a university in terms of its contribution to the knowledge economy, then Professor Bentley may seem to be right. If we distinguish between education and training and we believe that the former is an enterprise in which the young are initiated into the best that has been thought and written, then the marginalisation of specific knowledge might seem a little crass. Why does anyone choose to study a particular subject at university? Because, as Anthony O'Hear puts it:

They have a passion for and commitment to the questions and methods and content of the subject they are devoting themselves to. They believe that there are certain things worth studying for their own sake, because they enlighten us as to what we are, to what the world is and to what we might be: physics, mathematics, chemistry, biology, history, the social sciences, literature, the study of art, philosophy and theology. And they are right. These things are worth studying for their own sake, irrespective of any intellectual skills their study brings with them. But because they are the things the cleverest and most cultured people have, over the centuries, studied and worked on, their study is associated with intellectual abilities of a high order, and also with the most precious gift of all, the readiness to follow the truth wherever it might lead.

I think back to October 1965 when I went to Bristol University to read English. I was fortunate to have the poet Charles Tomlinson as my tutor. We would gather in his room for an hour or so on a Friday afternoon, and, as the lights came on in Berkley Square, we would read seventeenth-century literature with passion and commitment. It was exactly what I hoped university would be like. It is what I want future generations of students to experience and enjoy, whatever their subject might be. Hence my anger at the Government and those, like Professor Bentley, who have no understanding of what university study ought to involve.

Let us, however, park these minor disagreements and examine Professor Bentley's argument. We all agree that graduates should be able to communicate well and be able to solve problems and 'to critically analyse work', though some of us might also hope that somewhere they had learnt not to split infinitives. Actually, I think that they should be able to do these things before they are admitted to university. After all, undergraduates have spent thirteen years in formal education before embarking on their university studies and it is not unreasonable to expect them to have mastered the basic skills upon which learning depends. But is Professor Bentley right to isolate these 'skills' from the context in which they are taught and learnt? Take her own example of basketball. I am not quite sure what it is to 'analyse critically' in basketball, but let's assume that it has something to do with reading the pattern of play. Is this the same as analysing a literary text, or, a different skill again, a philosophical argument? It is not. The skill is subject specific. Bentley makes the same mistake that David Blunkett made when he demanded that all secondary school pupils should be taught 'thinking skills'. Thinking skills do not exist in a knowledge vacuum. We can think scientifically, historically, or philosophically. We cannot just think. The ability to think in any particular subject depends on a mastery of the knowledge that is specific to that subject. If you know nothing of the subject, you cannot identify the problem to be solved. You will not know what constitutes evidence. You will not be able to marshal that evidence into a persuasive and logical sequence. Knowledge of the subject does not, of course, mean that that logical sequence is necessarily achieved, but without it you do not have a chance.

It is easy to see why this silliness is so popular. Employers who, on occasion, have been rather too easily seduced by the buzz words and the rhetoric, complain that graduates do not possess 'the skills' they need. Keen to demonstrate their relevance to the real world, and to correct their anachronistic ways, universities have eagerly climbed aboard the skills bandwagon. Training? Education? They are the same thing, old boy. To argue that they are not is a dangerous game in which you are likely to be labelled an elitist snob, or, worse, as I have been, a fascist, on more than one occasion. Every current runs ever stronger in the same direction. If I have heard it once, I have heard it a hundred times. 'The besetting sin of our country is the failure to take vocational training seriously.' It is. We have failed to take vocational training seriously. The tragedy now, however, is that we believe that the only way to redeem ourselves is to blur the distinction between education and training, to marginalize the importance of specific subject knowledge and genuine academic disciplines, and in order, I suppose, to demonstrate to the world that vocational training is just as serious a business as academic education, to stuff what ought to be practical courses full of quasi-academic theorizing. It is a mess in which the aspirations of the politicians combine with the progressive ideology of many within the education establishment. It happened when grammar schools were swept away in the comprehensive revolution and we failed to think through the concept of the secondary modern. Now it is happening to higher education.

British universities were once admired throughout the world. What we have now is little more than a system of mass further education, with a nasty dose of anti-elitism thrown in. But, and this is the double whammy, this is further education that has turned its back on the useful in order to bask in the warm academic glow of spurious degrees of the kind listed above. More, as Kingsley Amis famously predicted, has meant worse.

The third way in which a government could hit its self-imposed target is to make university entrance easier. Surely not? Well, actually, yes. 'University entrance made easier to swell numbers': as *The Times* headline of 27 December 2000 announced, it is already happening. John O'Leary, *The Times* Education Editor, wrote that 'students are finding it easier to get university places as Tony Blair's expansion of higher education leads to lower offers by admissions officers'. Applications were up by some 3,000 over last year, but some 40,000 extra places had been funded by the Government. There simply were not enough students to go round. 'Even leading universities', O'Leary continued, were 'making lower offers'. Leeds, for example, was offering places on its combined language courses to students who had three E grades at A level. Inevitably, though, it is the new universities, the ex-polytechnics, that are experiencing the most acute recruitment difficulties. Some have had to face up to a real and significant drop in numbers. Lincolnshire and Humberside University has been forced to shut its original campus in Hull and focus most of its activities on the Lincoln site. In 1995–96, 9,840 undergraduates were studying business, engineering and applied social science at the former Humberside University. That number fell in the last academic year to just 6,614 students. This is, perhaps, a dramatic example, but O'Leary is surely right: 'the more that funding systems steer traditional universities towards the former polytechnics' natural territory, the less reason there is for students to go anywhere else'. And the greater the pressure on institutions that cannot fill vacant places to accept anyone who applies irrespective of their likely qualifications and ability to complete the course. Is it surprising that in the former polytechnics the average entry grade for physics and engineering courses is ten A level points and for mathematics and chemistry it is nine? There are many students on these courses with A level grades of two Es and a D. Some universities, it appears from press reports, are even accepting candidates who have no A level qualifications at all.

Significant numbers of students do not have the linguistic skills to cope with degree level work. In 1992, when around 20 per cent of the 18–21 age group were undertaking higher education, a survey by the Queen's English Society showed that lecturers from 148 departments across all disciplines considered some 20–30 per cent of their students to be poor in aspects of English. There is no reason to believe that things have improved since then. Will students who have problems with basic literacy and who know so little about their subjects that they scraped the lowest pass at A level benefit from their time at university? Some may, I suppose, deepen their understanding. If the university lays on sufficient remedial classes, some may perhaps leave able to read and write.

In the late eighties, 16 per cent of 18–21-year-olds were studying at universities or polytechnics. In the nineties, the polytechnics were designated universities and student numbers doubled. It would be nice if this expansion had been achieved without lowering standards, but academic after academic testifies to me the contrary. Here, for example, is Kevin Sharpe, Professor of History at Southampton University: 'Few first year students have any idea what constitutes even a basic argument and deliver three pages of simplistic narrative, based either on gleanings from an elementary text book or even more over-simplified lecture notes'. What we have now, he writes, is 'a culture of minimum intellectual demands' in which 'spoon-feeding (simplistic lectures, summary handouts, course packages, book lists with page numbers)' ensures that 'the whole university experience' is one in which students are 'infantilised'.

Is this what Mr Blair and Ms Morris want? They know that there is a continuing problem with literacy and numeracy in primary schools. They are so concerned at the failure of children to make progress in secondary school that they have introduced a multi-million pound initiative to 'transform' teaching and learning. Do they really think that this 'transformation' will happen overnight? To double the student population in a decade was to travel remarkably hopefully; to expect 50 per cent of the population to achieve a degree that represents the same standard of intellectual achievement as degrees in the past is simply silly.

Worse, it is cruel. The dropout rate from the University of North London is nearly 40 per cent. Could this have anything to do with the fact that this is a university that prides itself on its policy of accepting students with the poorest possible A level grades? The human cost of each student who drops out does not seem to matter to the university or to the Government, which, come hell or high water, is, determined to achieve its 50 per cent target.

There is no way out of this conundrum. If the Government wants more students with, in the words of Lord Dearing's report into Higher Education, 'more modest prior academic attainments or abilities' to be admitted to universities, then 'adaptations to programmes and qualifications will be needed'. For, 'if such changes are not made too many people will be set up to fail in higher education'. Higher education, in other words, has to be made less demanding so that students who are less able and less well-qualified can cope. So which way, Minister, are you going to jump? Are you going to let people fail or are you going to dumb the courses down? Or, third option, will you continue to whistle in the wind and pretend that intellectual rigour has been maintained and that open access is delivering New Labour's fabled Learning Age?

III

1. How many young people have the intellectual ability to benefit from a degree course?
2. How many graduates does the economy really need?
3. What is the difference between education and training?

The Government has either not asked itself these questions or has asked them and come up with the wrong answers.

The correct answers are as follows.

Question 1: More, certainly, than the 7 per cent that went to university in the sixties with Margaret Hodge and Graham Zellick, but the 35 per cent that are currently studying for a degree is too many, and, if a degree is to demand the same level of intellectual achievement as it did in the past, 50 per cent is for the foreseeable future an unrealistic aspiration.

Question 2: Far fewer than the Government would have us believe. Despite Ms Hodge's protestations to the contrary, our economic prosperity does not depend upon us educating more and more young people to degree level. She would do well to reflect that Germany has only 8.7 per cent of 18–21-year-olds on university courses. Greece has 28.9 per cent. She should listen to businessmen who are trying to recruit staff with craft qualifications and ensure that Further Education, which has for so long been the Cinderella service in the English education system, is resourced to meet these real skill shortages.

Question 3: Education is an enterprise in which the young engage with the best that has been thought and written. It has, to paraphrase Newman, no bearing upon any end external to itself. Training, which may, of course, involve the mastery of a significant body of knowledge, is, conversely, an activity in which the student is taught how to master the techniques and procedures needed to perform a particular task. It is not a very difficult distinction to grasp. The mystery is why so few people now seem to understand what Baroness Warnock meant when she wrote a few years ago that 'the test' of a 'real' university education is 'that students through their teachers should be conscious of standing on the edge of a developing and changing world of learning', why nobody understands that wholly vocational subjects (like Golf Course Management) are different from subjects which are either not vocational at all (like Medieval History) or are vocational with a strong academic content (like Law) and that it is only the latter subjects which should be studied in a university to degree level.

According to Harold MacMillan, J. A. Smith, Professor of Moral Philosophy at Oxford, greeted his new students with the following: 'Gentlemen, nothing that you will learn in the course of your studies will be of the slightest possible use to you in the after life – save only this – that if you work hard and intelligently you should be able to detect when a man is talking rot, and that, in my view, is the main, if not the sole purpose of education'.

That, if a university education has any purpose at all, seems to me to be about right.

CHAPTER 7

The Way Forward

I

Sticking plaster won't do. The wounds run too deep. The great and the good of the education establishment and the pundits of the left-leaning think tanks continue to undermine the very concept of education. A gullible government hangs on their every word. The talk, whatever the phrase might mean, is of 'radical modernisation'. The reality is that political commitment crumbles at the first whiff of union opposition. Does Mr Blair really want to involve the private sector in education? In all probability, he does. He does not suffer from the ideological hang-ups that afflict so many of his backbenchers and, indeed, ministers. He knows, come the next election, that he has to deliver the improvements in education he has promised for so long and that he cannot rely on state bureaucracy, local or national.

Fine, but he will have to stir himself. Nothing will happen without his personal involvement. Take last autumn's White Paper on the future of secondary education. The spin led everyone to believe that the great theme was to be private sector management of failing schools. In fact, the proposal was buried deep in the text at paragraph 6.23. Blink, and you missed it. Why? Because the unions, resolute in their antediluvian fervour and determined to pretend that all is well with our public services, or would be, if there was more investment and less wicked, demoralising talk of privatisation, had huffed and puffed. And, meanwhile, LEAs go on wasting public money, interfering in the running of schools, adding to the paper mountain that heads and teachers spend so much time trying to scale. University Departments of Education for their part do all they can to ensure that the next generation of teachers is committed to the thinking and values that, on any objective assessment, have done so much damage to our children's education. It is surgery, not sticking plaster, that is needed if standards in our schools are to rise as they can and must.

II

For the last thirty years I have been a cog in the local and national government machine. I taught. I trained teachers. I was Chief Inspector in Shropshire and Deputy Chief Education Officer in Devon and then Cornwall. I ran the National Curriculum Council and its successor body the School Curriculum and Assessment Authority. I was Chief Inspector of Schools for six years. I know, from personal experience, how most organisations within the education system function. Some, inevitably, are more effective than others. All have talented and committed staff who, often against the political and bureaucratic odds, make a positive contribution. The system as a whole, however, has not, does not and will not deliver. I wish I could come to a different judgement, but I cannot.

We have to face the facts. New Labour has, after all, pulled every possible lever. Their policies are, in my view, dangerously misguided, but I can only admire the energy and ingenuity Mr Blunkett and now Ms Morris have displayed. They have fiddled with every conceivable bit of the machine, servicing some parts and re-engineering others. And, yes, in some respects it functions more efficiently. More children learn to read. More know their tables. But 25 per cent of eleven-year-olds cannot and do not. Literacy and numeracy are Labour's greatest achievements. Turn to virtually any other aspect of the service and the story is the same: endless tinkering, massive investment leading to new bureaucracies, and little or no progress. Individual teachers and headteachers secure, of course, higher standards. They do so in spite of, not because of the frenzy of state activity that has engulfed them.

Readers who do not work in education will have no idea of the number of initiatives that teachers today are expected to implement. Pause for a moment, pour yourself a stiff gin and tonic and study this diagram which I reproduce courtesy of Tony Storey, who for the last thirty-one years has been headteacher of Hayfield School, Doncaster. Ignore the fact that the majority are not going to deliver very much. Reflect simply on the number of balls Tony Storey and his fellow heads are expected to keep in the air.

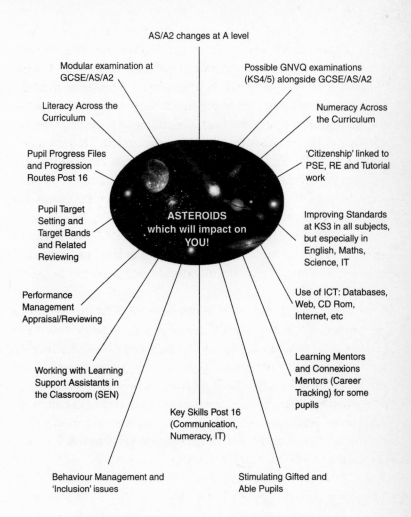

AS/A2 changes at A level

Modular examination at
GCSE/AS/A2

Possible GNVQ examinations
(KS4/5) alongside GCSE/AS/A2

Literacy Across the
Curriculum

Numeracy Across
the Curriculum

Pupil Progress Files
and Progression
Routes Post 16

'Citizenship' linked to
PSE, RE and Tutorial
work

Pupil Target
Setting and
Target Bands
and Related
Reviewing

ASTEROIDS
which will impact on
YOU!

Improving Standards
at KS3 in all subjects,
but especially in
English, Maths,
Science, IT

Performance
Management
Appraisal/Reviewing

Use of ICT: Databases,
Web, CD Rom,
Internet, etc

Working with Learning
Support Assistants in
the Classroom (SEN)

Learning Mentors
and Connexions
Mentors (Career
Tracking) for some
pupils

Key Skills Post 16
(Communication,
Numeracy, IT)

Behaviour Management and
'Inclusion' issues

Stimulating Gifted and
Able Pupils

God only knows when the penny will finally drop in Whitehall. But the lesson of these last five years is obvious. Politicians can only exhort and cajole, and, if they are feeling generous, invest. Educational bureaucrats are not omnipotent. Professors of education are far from omniscient. External intervention is not going to work. Estelle Morris, as Secretary of State in this desperately interventionist government, has a very clear decision to make. She can keep digging or she can reduce the amount of state regulation of and interference in schools, and, what is equally important, take steps to empower parents as consumers and create a proper market in education.

Don't hold your breath. For all the talk of deregulation and 'earned autonomy' (which means that if Tony Storey does not want to follow a particular regulation he has to ask the Secretary of State if he can be excused), the approach is not going to change. The hole, therefore, can only get deeper. Why? Because schools and teachers cannot cope; because Whitehall cannot rule twenty-four thousand schools; because, when it comes to the crunch, the political will tends to evaporate; and, the most fundamental reason of all, because Ms Morris is, in my judgement, likely to listen to advisers who will persuade her to promote policies that will make matters worse, not better.

It is not simply the fact that there are so many schools that makes the logistics so daunting. The infrastructure simply is not there. The Standards and Effectiveness Unit seems, I know, to double in size month by month and the back pages of the *Times Educational Supplement* are full of advertisements for advisers in this and consultants in that. The troops are, nonetheless, thin on the ground. When I was an adviser in Shropshire back in the 1980s I was responsible for the teaching of English in forty-odd secondary and over two hundred primary schools. It was a tall order. Conferences can be held. Visits can be made, albeit infrequently, to a few schools. One-off contact is never, though, going to achieve real change. Many of the academics and administrators upon whom reforming politicians have to rely are, moreover, likely to be opposed to the policies they are expected to implement. The reform process can be hijacked all too quickly and easily. It happened with the National Curriculum. It is the biggest problem, as I have admitted, that OFSTED faced and faces. How to effect change when the agents of change are part of the culture that needs to be changed? This is the conundrum upon which every centralised initiative over the last couple of decades has foundered. Estelle Morris, for all her optimistic talk of 'partnership', is unlikely to find an answer.

Indeed, her commitment to partnership is part of the problem. Reform worth having is bound to provoke resistance. Yes, I know, everything depends upon the willingness of teachers to implement new ideas. But there is a huge gap between the apolitical pragmatism of most members of the teaching profession and the negativity of The Blob, as the US Education Secretary so memorably labelled the education establishment. The Blob's resistance to change has to be tackled head on, and this, on the evidence of her past performance, Estelle Morris is unlikely to do. After all, she was the minister responsible for the introduction of what was meant to be a system of performance pay. Look what happened. Time and time again, it was Estelle Morris who took the decision not to contract out the services of LEAs failed by Ofsted. What is the point, colleagues in OFSTED used to ask, in spending so much time and energy on these LEA inspections, when nothing ever seems to happen?

The answer, I suppose, was that they concentrated a few minds and revealed something of the bureaucracy and waste that is to be found in too many local authorities. They did not, that is, do any harm. Ms Morris's overall programme of reform most certainly will. The bombardment from above has already demoralised and wearied teachers. It has distracted them from their classroom responsibilities. Worse, as I have argued throughout this book, if the ideas that drive the reform programme are woolly and wrongheaded (and for the most part they are), then that programme will simply inflict further damage on an already damaged education system. Ms Morris's lack of political grit might, come to think of it, prove to be rather a good thing.

To argue that ministers should abandon their hyperactive 'crusade' to raise standards is not, however, to suggest that we should return to the good old, pre-National Curriculum, pre-OFSTED days so beloved of trade union general secretaries. Indeed, a couple of caveats are probably needed before I discuss what it might mean to encourage the development of a market that empowers parents.

The first is personal. I have never, I admit, been a great fan of state interference into our private or collective lives. The more avaricious the tentacles of state control, the less freedom we have to manage our own affairs. Freedom brings a sense of responsibility that, in turn, leads to personal and professional satisfaction. This satisfaction is, I believe, a very precious good. But the conclusion I have reached on the role that the state should play in the provision and running of schools stems more from a study of the evidence than from any prior personal or political conviction. If I thought that local or national government had stopped the rot, my conclusion would be different. In this sense, if no other, I am solidly New Labour: what matters in these post-ideological times is, as Mr Blair likes to tell us, what works. The state does not. If anything, it has quickened the rot.

The second is a defence of OFSTED and, indeed, myself, against the charge that inspection is the agency of state control par excellence. It is not. On the one hand, there is Labour's determination to run things from Whitehall, to micro-manage twenty-four thousand schools through regulation and diktat. On the other, there is the belief that having specified the requirements of the National Curriculum, schools should be free to decide how they can best meet those requirements and should then be held accountable for their performance. OFSTED is the agent of that accountability. I admit that, in practice, some inspectors exceeded their brief and judged schools against their own individual sense of the educational or management good, but this was something that, as Chief Inspector, I always condemned. The Inspectorate exists to describe what is happening in schools, what, for better or worse, is being achieved, not to encourage compliance and the argument that I am about to advance does not represent a radical departure from the thinking that underpinned my time at OFSTED.

III

So: standards will rise when The Blob is finally wrestled to the ground. It is that simple and that daunting. Will it happen? It could, if the political will were there. But it is not. The Blob can for the moment breathe easy. There is no real threat.

The Liberal Democrat spokesman on education, an ex-head-teacher and anti-OFSTED cheer leader called Phil Willis, is in my opinion a fully paid up member of The Blob. His recipe for improvement? Praise more. Tax more. Invest more. I can only say that I wish it were this simple. Does more money mean better grades? In real terms we spend about three times more on education than we did forty years ago. More students now achieve top grades. Phil Willis and his fellow Lib Dems jump to what seems to be the obvious conclusion. I would advise caution. Why did results rocket in 1987/8? Could it have had anything to do with the introduction of GCSE? Why a decade or so earlier did they level off? Could this be because so many grammar schools were abolished at that time? Might (remember the discussion in Chapter 1 of how examinations have changed over the years) grade inflation be as potent an explanation as increased funding? Don't misunderstand me. I am not advocating that we should spend less on education. A wise government would certainly do all it could to improve inadequate school buildings. It would think how it might pay effective teachers more, particularly if they are working in demanding schools. It would also, however, take a long hard look at how the existing budget might deliver better value for money. In education, as in any other industry, it is how the money is used that matters, not the size of the sum that is invested. It is obvious. I could take Phil Willis to schools where a munificent government could quadruple the budget overnight and it would not make a jot of difference. Why? Because the leadership is not there, the management is inefficient, the expectations low, the teaching poor. Investment is not, in itself, the answer.

Labour, for its part, wants, as ever, to have it all ways. The Prime Minister talks of private sector investment while his Secretary of State espouses the warm virtues of 'partnership'. Well, which is it to be? When will our politicians ever learn? When will they understand that The Blob knows which side its bread is buttered. It makes, as always, the right noises. Excellence in Cities? Yes, of course, an excellent initiative. 'Earned autonomy' for successful schools? Brilliant, just what we have always wanted. And, in reality, the idea will be swallowed up and stifled. Time and again it has happened. Time and again it will happen. Take the fundamental issue of bureaucracy. Ms Morris will never stem the deluge of directives that swamps schools until she tackles the bureaucracy responsible for that deluge. It ought, by now, to be clear that the bureaucracy is the problem and that bureaucrats are no more likely to vote for real change than turkeys for Christmas. But, if the Prime Minister sort of understands, Estelle Morris, it seems, does not: The Blob is more powerful now than it was in 1997, and all the signs are that it is set in this Parliament to become yet more powerful.

Would a Conservative victory at the next election change things? Traditionally, of course, the Conservative Party has always been sceptical of the state and committed to the defence of individual freedom and consumer choice. A future Conservative Government ought to constitute as serious a threat to The Blob as previous Conservative administrations did in the late 1980s and early '90s. Indeed, it should finish the job that the two Kenneths, Baker and Clarke, began. At the time of writing, however, Damian Green, the new spokesman on education, was feeling his way. No Conservative values or beliefs, however core, however traditional, can, it seems, be taken for granted. There is an understandable fear that any mention of privatisation will be used by New Labour spin doctors to frighten the electorate and alienate yet more potential Conservative voters. Personally, I believe that the logic of the case is so powerful and the degree of dissatisfaction so profound, that there is little to lose and everything to gain. The Conservative Party needs, that is, to connect with the frustrations and aspirations of parents throughout middle England. It ought to have the courage of its traditional Conservative convictions. This may, however, prove to be too radical a view for these modernising times.

IV

The Blob is likely, therefore, to survive for a while yet. Let us, nonetheless, travel hopefully. Let us assume that whichever Party wins the next election it understands the problem and has the courage to act upon it. What then? What needs to be done, on the one hand, to counter the bureaucracy and waste and ideological silliness, and, on the other, to empower parents and stimulate an educational market?

It is not, on the former, a matter of stronger leadership and more intelligent management. We have had reform after reform of local government and virtually nothing has been achieved. So, too, in Whitehall. You would think, reading its latest *Departmental Report*, that the DfES has faced up to any problems it may have experienced in the past and transformed itself into a formidably efficient organisation. It has, after all, been awarded 'Central Government Beacon Status' for its 'leadership' and 'learning'. It has taken steps 'to ensure that its policy making is joined-up, based on evidence, and evaluated properly'. It prides itself on its 'joined-up' (a key New Labour value, as we all know) approach to 'customer service' and has set up a 'central benchmarking and excellence unit to co-ordinate [yes, you have guessed it] benchmarking activity and promote and facilitate [whatever this might be] the European Foundation for Quality Model'. It has 'developed and introduced a multimedia masters degree in leadership and published a leadership handbook'. It submitted its 'business planning process to peer review' and, yes, you have probably guessed it again, the review 'concluded that the planning process worked well'. If this sounds cynical, it is. I know from personal experience that, in this through-the-looking-glass world, the louder and more complacent the self-congratulation, the more threadbare the actual performance is likely to be. The DfES is an organisation that is obsessed with processes and procedures. It has embraced every conceivable management fad, but remains damagingly hierarchical, and, bogged in a mire of non-communication, it is both hopelessly sluggish in its identification of priorities and incoherent in the formulation of policy.

The private sector has, I admit, its problems, but the DfES, like many other government departments, simply would not survive in the real world. Government departments do not go bankrupt. Civil servants rarely, if ever, get fired. Nobody really knows who is responsible for what. Suppose 80 per cent of eleven-year-olds do achieve Level 4 in English by 2002. Should the Secretary of State take any credit? Which of his officials made the difference? Or, on the other hand, do we conclude that the triumph is the teachers? And, conversely, if they do not, then who should take the blame? It will not, of course, be Mr Blunkett, who famously promised to resign if the target was not hit. He has moved on to higher things, as he knew he would. But actually it does not matter. The murk is so dense, the non-accountability so absolute, that meaningful answers to these questions are impossible.

It is all words. Departmental Objective 1 is to ensure that 'all young people reach sixteen with the skills, attitudes and personal qualities that will give them a secure foundation for lifelong learning, work and citizenship in a rapidly changing world'. Objective 2 is even woollier: The Department is aiming to develop 'in everyone a commitment to lifelong learning, so as to enhance their lives, improve their employability in a changing labour market and create the skills that our economy and employers need'. Aspirations as cosmic as these are not susceptible to rational review. They are a smokescreen behind which a huge, unaccountable and highly inefficient organisation hides.

The Prime Minister knows this, and, from time to time, complains about how the Civil Service is failing to promote his programme of reform. Indeed, he has recently let it be known that in future Permanent Secretaries will, without exception, be appointed from outside the Civil Service. Quite what he thinks this will do for morale and how he expects to recruit super-managers from the private sector, I am not sure, but you could hardly have a clearer statement of prime ministerial dissatisfaction.

The problem is not, though, primarily or even mainly one of people. An awful lot of DfES officials are certainly stuck in their bureaucratic rut. Senior civil servants can be terribly arrogant in a Yes, Ministerish sort of way, and many would find it taxing (and, no doubt, a mite demeaning) to soil their Oxbridge hands on the tedium of the management detail. Will top quality private sector managers want to work with hyperactive ministers who are more interested in establishing their own reputations than they are in the practicality and good sense of the initiatives they expect their civil servants to implement? Policy making in the DfES is not, I am afraid, 'joined-up, based on evidence and evaluated properly'. Take the flagship policy Excellence in Cities, which cost £23 million in 1999–2000. The Departmental Report admits that, I quote, 'it is early days' and that the only evidence of the initiative achieving anything is the fact that 'secondary schools in the first Excellence in Cities areas are improving faster than schools elsewhere measured by the percentage of pupils gaining five GCSEs or GNVQs at A* to C' – which is scarcely surprising given the low baseline from which the Excellence in Cities schools started. Did this lack of evidence and any proper evaluation cause ministers to proceed with caution? Far from it, £80 million is to be invested in this ragbag of wing-and-a-prayer activities in the year 2000–01. I cannot see many private sector managers wanting to section themselves voluntarily.

It is not better leadership the DfES needs. It is reform that begins with the recognition that this is a bloated empire that has no legitimate function. The money currently used to fund ministerial initiatives would be better spent in schools. Here are some examples: £235 million was spent in 2000–01 on reducing class sizes. The headteacher may or may not want to reduce class sizes. Many, for very sensible reasons, do not want. In a sane world they would be able to decide what to do with their extra cash. Over a billion pounds is tied up in the so-called 'Standards Fund'. Headteachers have to bid for their share of the cake. They may not want to implement the centrally determined initiatives the fund is designed to promote. That is hard luck. The political will is deemed more important than the good sense of the man or woman who is in a position to know what needs doing in a particular school. Education Action Zones? This initiative, which ministers themselves now acknowledge to have failed, has this year (2001) eaten up another £60 million. 'Modernising the teaching profession', performance pay to you and me, the debacle by which every teacher who applied to go through the 'threshold' was awarded an extra £2,000 a year for life, another £737 million. And so the list goes on. These are not initiatives that are going to transform standards in our schools. They have been dreamt up by advisers who, more often than not, view the realities of classroom life through the prism of educational theory and political ideology. They are costly to implement. They tend, predictably enough, to spawn new bureaucracies. And they offend against what ought to be the most basic tenet of all: namely, that taxpayers' money should be devolved to the school so that it can be used in classrooms to educate our children. It is the headteacher who should decide how it is used. He or she should then be held accountable. End of story, and why not? We do not need the DfES in anything approaching its present shape and size.

Neither, for the reasons given in Chapter 5, do we need LEAs. The school is in the best position to determine what support it needs and from whom it wants to purchase it. Headteachers are paid to run their schools. Let them do it. They complain about bureaucratic interference. It is time for ministers to acknowledge and act upon the obvious truth: the interference will stop when and only when those who are paid to interfere lose their jobs.

There are, as I have acknowledged, management issues, such as home/school transport and some aspects of special educational needs, which are best not devolved to the individual school. Of course, and it ought not to be beyond the wit of man to devise new ways of delivering these services. So, too, with the other argument that is often put in support of the LEA: that successful schools may well be able to run their own affairs, but we need a body to intervene and support the schools that are not capable of managing their own destiny. Indeed we do, but it is not the LEA. OFSTED's annual analysis of the test and examination data will trigger an early inspection if a school's results look to be declining. Parents, moreover, are to be encouraged to ask for an inspection if they are worried about what is going on in their child's school. The identification of failure is not, therefore, a problem and to have OFSTED and the LEA paddling in the same pool is a waste of resources and a recipe for management confusion. The job of dealing with the school that has failed involves technical and professional expertise that can and should be provided by the market. OFSTED lets contracts for the inspection of schools. It ought, logically, to let contracts for school improvement.

Once again it is a big step for any political party to take. To abolish local education authorities is, after all, to remove a shield that national politicians have, understandably enough, liked to hide behind when the going gets tough. 'Your school does not have enough money to mend the boiler/employ a new teacher/buy a new set of science textbooks? How dreadful! The problem is the inefficiency of your LEA. We're spending far more on education than the Conservatives/Labour ever did and doing everything possible to solve problems . . .'. And, vice versa, of course, on the LEA side. Will the national politicians ever be prepared to upset their local colleagues upon whom, when it comes to elections, they depend? Probably not. But the financial and management logic is clear. Unnecessary bureaucracy, of which there is as much in local government as there is in national, should be eliminated. Every penny of available resource should be pushed down into classrooms so that children benefit directly. The head and his or her teachers should be trusted to do the job, rewarded when they succeed and fired if they fail.

If the DfES were to be slimmed down radically and LEAs in their present form abolished, we would not only save billions of pounds of taxpayers' money. We would, and in the long run this may be an even more important consequence, have taken a very significant step towards eliminating the lunacy of learnacy and other equally wacky ideas. What, though, of other organisations that have from time to time flirted with the false progressive gods? These are the teacher training institutions, the Qualifications and Curriculum Authority and last but, in the context of this difficult issue, certainly not least, OFSTED.

Let us begin with teacher training. In 1997, a retired Australian academic, Geoffrey Partington, conducted a number of interviews with leading academics in teacher training institutions. His conclusion makes depressing reading.

Although the amount of time available for educational theory of any kind was much less in 1997 than 1979, I found that New Left proselytising was as intense as ever in some of the remaining areas in which it could be practised. Nothing could be less true than that Conservative governments had carried out an ideological purge of their own during their years of office. New Left ideological zeal flourished most of all in ubiquitous courses claiming to counter sexism or racism or to promote equal opportunities, but it also powerfully influenced many of the curriculum courses which had survived the attenuation of the disciplines of education and generic educational studies. Curriculum courses in science and mathematics, reading and literacy were as likely to show the signs of New Left hegemony as were history or social studies.

'Ideological zeal' is exactly the right phrase. Here is just one example. Mairtin Mac an Ghaill lectures at the University of Sheffield School of Education. He is 'an authority on "schooling masculinities" or how "schooling processes can be seen to form gendered identities, marking out correct or appropriate styles of being'. He believes, apparently, that 'comprehensive reorganis-ation, child-centred pedagogy, anti-racism and anti-sexism are key elements of the modernist project, informed by a belief in collectivism, humanism and rational progression and social jus-tice'. What, you might well ask, does this dubious utopianism have to do with initiating a novice teacher into the hard realities of the craft of the classroom? My answer is unprintable. The reading lists Geoffrey Partington reviewed rarely referred to 'any writer who could in educational terms be described as "New Right", "Old Right", Conservative or Liberal'. Some lists in essential subjects like the teaching of literacy were 'indefensibly unbalanced'. Many science courses had been 'subjected to ideo-logical takeover by radical Constructivism', a relativist and subjectivist epistemology that denies the possibility of objective knowledge.

Partington paints a damning picture of 'ideological capture'. Not all teacher training, of course, reflects bias of this kind, but too much does. Buy any copy of the *Times Educational Supplement* and the odds are that you will find an article by a professor of education espousing his or her vision of what edu-cation ought to involve. More often than not, such articles will be hostile to what the government of the day, Conservative or Labour, it does not seem to matter which, is trying to achieve. This, in itself, ought to give ministers pause for thought. Does Estelle Morris really think she is going to harness these academics to her programme of reform? Or does she, deep down, share their progressive, romantic longings?

The answer is that it is probably a bit of both: arrogance on the one hand and recidivism on the other. She has certainly never been a fan of what to my mind is the best and most commonsensical approach to teacher training – the apprenticeship of student teachers to good classroom teachers in what is known as School Centred Teacher Training (SCITT) initiatives. Predictably enough, the very word 'apprenticeship' raises the ire of many teacher trainers. Professor Colin Richards, for example, who was once a middle-ranking HMI, and colleagues from St Martin's College, Lancaster, complain that the Government's National Curriculum for Initial Teacher Training gives 'little or no recognition . . . to the importance of critically examining the meaning and purpose of education, understanding child development, holding up the school National Curriculum to critical scrutiny, or to studying the social, cultural and ethical dimensions of teaching and learning in primary schools'. It is all, of course, an attempt to bolster insecure academic egos, though I have to admit that the National Curriculum for ITT and other similar top-down attempts to impose some common sense into this arcane and self-indulgent world have not really achieved that much.

The way forward, whatever the Secretary of State might think, is to encourage more SCITTs and gradually to phase out all university teacher training. SCITTs after all now occupy five out of the top ten places in the annual table of teacher training institutions prepared by Alan Smithers and Pamela Robinson of Liverpool University's Centre for Education and Employment

Research. The table ranks teacher training providers on the entry qualifications and employment record of their students and their OFSTED inspection grades. It is obvious really. The best way to train the teachers of tomorrow is alongside the best teachers of today.

The QCA is important because it is responsible for the National Curriculum, the administration of National Curriculum tests, and the maintenance of standards in public examinations. Like the DfES, it is over-staffed, and, like the DfES, a good number of its senior officers are less than committed to a traditional concept of education. It is the problem I have commented on before: politicians need professionals to work through the detail and implement their reforms, but most senior figures in the world of education, however cleverly they hide the fact at interview, are enthusiastic supporters of the status quo that the Government wants to change. The situation may have improved since the early nineties when I was Chief Executive of the National Curriculum Council and the School Curriculum and Assessment Authority, the two bodies that preceded the QCA, but somehow I doubt it. In those days it was desperately difficult to find staff who were both up to the job professionally and sympathetic to the Government's programme of reform. There were a number of honourable exceptions, but I can remember spending far too much time cutting gobbledegook out of incomprehensible policy proposals and trying to persuade people to focus on the subject knowledge the National Curriculum was meant to embody. Too many staff remained deeply committed to fashionable progressive approaches. More generally, there was a feeling that subjects were themselves an anachronism that should be replaced by cross-curricular skills and themes. Given the fact that many of the great and the good appointed to the Board were as unsound in their educational views as the staff they were meant to lead, the marvel, looking back, is that the curriculum which emerged was not more flawed.

The odds then and, I am certain, now are stacked against QCA doing the job it ought to be doing. It has not the right staff. It has a Board that includes Ted Wragg, Professor of Education at Exeter University, who once told me that he intended to 'blow the National Curriculum out of the water', and who has not, I imagine, changed his views. It has never achieved a proper independence from ministers and their officials. The introduction of Citizenship was a good example of this latter problem. Few, if any, senior members of the Authority approved of the Secretary of State's Citizenship proposals. Nobody, however, thought it a good idea to mount any public opposition. This may well, given Mr Blunkett's determination to have his own way, have been the sensible decision. The failure to speak out, though, does prompt the obvious rhetorical question: is there any point in spending millions of pounds a year of taxpayers' money on an agency which rubber stamps the Secretary of State's personal enthusiasms?

The more fundamental question is whether we need a National Curriculum at all. When Ted Wragg and I discussed the National Curriculum back in 1989, I asked him whether his constant *Times Educational Supplement* sniping helped the teachers who had to implement the new subject Orders. At that time, I was convinced that the National Curriculum was an important and positive initiative. Visiting schools in three different local education authorities, I had become increasingly disturbed by the eccentricity of local provision. The curriculum children studied ought not, it seemed to me, to depend upon the whims of their teachers. They should be taught the same range of subjects wherever they went to school. Too many girls were dropping science just as quickly as they could; too many boys were opting out of foreign languages. Expectations in too many schools were too low, in some cases hopelessly so. A National Curriculum that articulated what it was reasonable to expect children to know at different points in their school careers would, assuming we defined expectations appropriately, challenge teachers who never stretched their pupils. It was, surely, a good idea to try to define what constituted progress in different subjects? Take my own subject, English. I used to ask my eleven-year-olds and my sixteen-year-old pupils to write stories. I had no clear idea what progress the older students should have made. A story was a story was a story. If I was vague, I am sure other teachers were, too. Greater clarity would help, I thought, both teachers and pupils.

Professor Wragg disagreed. The National Curriculum, he thought, was wrong in principle in that politicians were telling teachers what to do. This is not, for the reasons I gave in Chapter 3, a concern that I shared. The argument that every teacher must as a matter of principle define their own curriculum has always seemed to me absurd. Indeed, this ridiculous belief has, I believe, done more to exacerbate the teacher workload problem than anything else. A teacher's professionalism depends upon their ability to explain and inspire, not upon their freedom to seize serendipitously on whatever catches their or their pupils' attention.

I have not changed my mind. Ted Wragg still seems to me hopelessly and unhelpfully romantic in his approach. I have lost faith in the principle of a National Curriculum for other, more serious reasons. I recognise that the argument for its retention remains powerful. We need, don't we, more perhaps than ever before, a statement of what education ought to involve? The National Curriculum is the thin blue line, a last defence against the barbarian, skill obsessed hordes. The situation, so the argument goes, has deteriorated to a point where we can rely neither on the producers nor the consumers. The former, trained in universities which despise a concern for the transmission of knowledge as a Gradgrindian anachronism, want to jettison subjects in favour of cross-curricular themes and transferable skills; the latter neither understand nor care, and, if they do, they are impotent when it comes to confronting the sophistry of the professional.

The thin blue line argument would be persuasive if the National Curriculum was a final defence. But, sadly, it is not. This is a debate where the judgement depends as much on the reality of the current situation as the principle of the argument. The National Curriculum is under attack from all sides. There is little reason to believe that Ms Morris and her ministers are about to recognise the error of their progressive ways and leap belatedly to its defence. The prospect now is of a curriculum that enshrines the evils it was meant to defeat, and that is not a good scenario. The rats will continue to gnaw away. It is a lost cause.

This is the first reason why, reluctantly, I have come to the conclusion that the National Curriculum should be abolished. The second sits uneasily with the inflammatory language I have just employed. I believe, passionately and absolutely, that our children should have access to a curriculum that is rooted in the belief that what matters is the best that has been thought and known. Others, like, for example, Ted Wragg, do not. It hurts to come to this conclusion, but those who want their children to be taught Wragg's (I joke not) 'cubic curriculum' or any other equally bizarre version of the educational good, ought to be able to send their unfortunate offspring to a school which bases its teaching on the chosen approach, however eccentric it might be. I used to believe that the state had a duty to protect children from the 'wrong' sort of education. If public money was involved, then the education provided ought to be as good an education as we could make it. It was all right for Summerhill, A S Neill's infamous, progressive school in Suffolk, to pursue its

Academically successful schools are, more often than not, schools which offer their pupils a rich range of cultural and sporting opportunities. There is nothing wrong with teaching to the test if the test is testing a curriculum worth learning. No, we need to know whether individual children are progressing as they should and whether individual schools are ensuring that their pupils realise their academic potential. The latter information is critical if a proper market in education is to develop.

Who, though, is to administer the tests and monitor public examinations if the QCA is to be abolished? The DfES could obviously enough take on the job, and, given the fact that the QCA has failed either to establish its independence from the department or to protect standards against the grade inflation that has so devalued the examination currency, this might be the way forward. The logical move, however, would be to transfer responsibility to OFSTED. This may sound like posthumous empire building, but OFSTED is the body responsible for educational standards, and, in principle, if not always in practice, it is completely independent of the DfES. That independence was thought by Parliament in 1992 to be vital with regard to the freedom to report the inspection evidence without fear or favour. Exactly the same argument ought, obviously, to apply to test and examination data. Ministers have too much of a vested interest to be allowed anywhere near public examinations.

V

Last autumn, I was invited to talk at the Education Leaders Conference in Atlanta, Georgia. In preparation, I read the report that the United States National Committee on Excellence in Education published back in 1983. Two sentences made me stop and reflect on our own approach to education reform: 'If an unfriendly foreign power had attempted to impose on America the mediocre education performance that exists today, we might well have viewed it as an act of war. As it stands, we have allowed this to happen to ourselves'. That is honest, I thought, and honesty has always seemed to me to be the first and crucial step if we are serious about raising standards.

It is one that we in this country are increasingly reluctant to take. Many headteachers and most Labour and Liberal Democrat politicians think that the only sensible tactic is to play the problems down and talk the morale up. 'We don't criticise our children all the time', headteachers used to say to me when I was Chief Inspector. 'If we did, their confidence would be undermined and they would never learn anything.' Why, they asked me, could I not understand this basic psychology? They had a point. Self-confidence is important. Self-delusion, however, can be a problem, and, listening to Estelle Morris on the radio this morning, I wondered whether she understood the gap between her rhetoric and the reality in too many schools, and, if she did, whether it might not be better if she were to be, just once in a while, a little more honest.

Mind you, it took the Americans a long while to realise what they needed to do. I quote from *An Education Agenda*, a fascinating report on a joint project into parental choice run by the National Centre for Policy Analysis and Children First America:

The experts said we should decrease class size, so across America we did, by 10 per cent since 1982.

The experts said we should increase teachers' salaries, so we did.

The experts said we ought to begin teaching children earlier, so we did that too, through mandatory kindergarten. Now 12 states and the District of Columbia require children to attend kindergarten, and another 24 require local school districts to offer kindergarten although attendance is not mandatory.

The experts said we had to spend money – and, oh my, did we spend money. Since 1980, spending on education across America has grown half as fast as inflation (education expenditure per student is up 194 per cent; inflation up 123 per cent).

So for all our time, for all our efforts, for all of this cash register mentality, just what have we accomplished? Sadly, not much.

Half of our high school seniors cannot identify Robert E Lee or locate France on a map. SAT exams taken by above-average students have dropped 80 points in 30 years. On international math and science tests, American students score 12th best in the world. Since 1980, NAEP reading and math scores have remained static. In some of our worst schools, the dropout rate exceeds 50 per cent'.

In America as in England, the experts continue to demand more investment in education. They defend the status quo and they dream up one top-down initiative after another. But in America, unlike in England, there is now a real commitment to making parental choice a reality. We have a lot to learn.

If we want standards to rise it is not enough to slim down the DfES, abolish teacher training institutions, the Qualifications and Curriculum Authority and LEAs in their current form. These reforms would complete the job the Conservatives began in 1988. They would solve the problem of regulation and bureaucracy overload and ensure that taxpayers' money was used where most taxpayers want and expect it to be used: in school classrooms. Above all, they would tackle the flow of anti-educational ideas that has damaged so much of state education.

So far, so good, and action of this kind would certainly clear the ground.

But the next stage is to face up to the fact that politicians of all parties have wittered on for too long about parental choice. The reality, as so many parents know, is that there is no choice. There is, of course, if you can afford to educate your child privately or move house so that you live in the right catchment area. If you cannot, you have had it. Flying back from America, I read and reread the chapter Virginia Walden contributed to *An Education Agenda*. 'Why', she asked, 'do urban schools do such a poor job of educating minority students?' And she went on to answer her own question in two brief, blunt and desperately important sentences: 'Because they can. Low income parents have nowhere else to go, and the school districts have a captive audience'. Waiting for my bag to appear on the conveyor belt, I suddenly thought how interesting it would be to lock Estelle Morris and her ministers into an examination hall for a couple of hours and ask them to ponder Ms Walden's question. '"Why do urban schools do such a poor job of educating minority pupils? Because they can". Discuss'. The answers would, I think, make fascinating reading.

If I were tackling this assignment, my essay would begin with Milton Friedman. Friedman believes that the American education system needs to be 'radically reconstructed'. That reconstruction, he argues, can only be achieved through privatisation. 'A private, for profit industry' must be encouraged to develop that will 'provide a wide variety of learning opportunities and effective competition to public schools'. He recognises that this reconstruction 'cannot come about overnight' and suggests that 'the most sensible way to bring about a gradual yet substantial transformation from government to private enterprise is to enact in each state a voucher system that enables parents to choose freely the schools their children attend'. This transformation will only happen, however, if the introduction of vouchers creates 'a large demand for private schools' and 'a real incentive' for 'entrepreneurs to enter the industry'. The voucher must therefore be 'universal, available to all who are now entitled to send their children to government schools' and 'large enough to cover the costs of a private profit-making school offering a high quality education'. It is essential that 'no conditions be attached to the acceptance of vouchers that interfere with the freedom of private enterprises to experiment, to explore and to innovate'.

I believe that he is right. In England, vouchers, like markets, are a dirty word for many educationalists and most, if not all, left-wing politicians. Their antipathy is understandable, for as Friedman writes: 'Nothing else will destroy . . . the power of the current educational establishment – a necessary pre-condition for radical improvement in our education system. And nothing else will provide the public (i.e. state) schools with the competition that will force them to improve in order to hold their clientele'. But, and it is a very big but, everybody else – 'parents, students, dedicated teachers, taxpayers – for whom the cost of the education system will decline' – would benefit if a system of vouchers were to be introduced. And, of course, it is those, like Virginia Walden, who live in inner-city districts where there is no choice of school, that would benefit the most.

The first objection to vouchers turns this last point on its head. 'Rubbish', the unions and the left sneer dismissively, 'it is the child from a disadvantaged background that would suffer if a right-wing government were ever to be so stupid as to bring in any such elitist, divisive system. Vouchers would simply make it easier for white, middle-class families to withdraw their children from state schools. What chance then would there be of providing equal educational opportunity to the children left behind?' To which the reply is that the equality of educational opportunity that matters so much to the left is in reality a sick joke. The majority of inner-city schools offer a desperately inadequate education. Most parents who can afford to do so already send their children to private schools or move to more affluent areas where education is better. Poor families cannot do this. They have no choice. Did Mr Blair send his children to the local comp? Does *Guardian* editor Alan Rushbridger? Did David Blunkett's educational guru, Michael Barber? I could fill the page with the names of the great and the good who wax lyrical about the professionalism and commitment and achievement of state teachers whilst simultaneously reaching deep into their pockets to pay for their own children's private education. The idea that less affluent families might, through a voucher scheme, have access to the same opportunities they enjoy is, it seems, totally unacceptable. There is no equality of opportunity. The system as it exists today is desperately unfair. What is truly unacceptable is the hypocrisy of those who bang their socialist drum in support of equality of opportunity, knowing that the privilege of their position means that they will never, thank you very much, have to expose their own children to the day-to-day reality of a failing inner-city school. It stinks.

More to the empirical point, the American experience shows that the children of the disadvantaged and the poor do benefit. Consider these findings from the Milwaukee, Cleveland and San Antonio voucher programmes. Families are only entitled to vouchers if they earn less than $30,433 a year and are therefore below the official 'poverty' line. The average income for families in Cleveland is $18,750 a year. In San Antonio it is $15,990 a year. In Milwaukee it is a mere $10,860 – the average family could triple its income and still retain official poverty status. 'Choice families', as Daniel McGroarty writes, 'are among the poorest of the poor'. The conclusion is the same whatever the statistics you choose to employ. Family status? Seventy-six per cent of Milwaukee voucher students live in single parent female-headed households. In Cleveland, the figure is 70 per cent. Neither is it true that voucher schools cream off the academic elite. Voucher students, for example, from the Edgewood district of San Antonio have much the same mathematics scores as other students in the district. Their reading scores are slightly higher, but still by national standards very low. They were as likely to have been suspended from school during the previous year as any other student.

In my opinion, Milton Friedman is right. Vouchers should be made available to all parents, irrespective of the family income. Why, after all, should anyone, however wealthy, pay twice for their child's education? But a voucher scheme does not, as these American schemes demonstrate, have to subsidise, as the critics would have it, the middle class. It could, if this is what the Government wanted, be limited to those families who are living in poverty and who currently have no choice but to send their children to a failing school.

Forced to admit this obvious truth, opponents of vouchers turn to other objections. They assert, for example, in a deeply patronising fashion, that, if they can be bothered to think about the voucher opportunity at all, poor families are unlikely to be able to exercise a sensible, well-informed choice. Here again, there are lessons to be learnt from America.

Nearly 60 per cent of the San Antonio parents who had chosen to send their children to a voucher school did so because they thought they would receive better teaching. Parents in New York chose voucher schools because of 'teacher quality, what is taught in class, safety, school discipline, school quality and class size'. Interestingly, they were not particularly concerned about the school's location, whether or not the child had friends at the school, or the quality of the sports programme. So much for the inability of the poor to make an intelligent choice.

Won't vouchers leave state schools with an ineducable rump of children whose parents don't give a damn? To repeat: the American experience shows that vouchers do not cream off the best students. Having reviewed eight different evaluations of six voucher schemes by four different research teams, Jay Greene concluded that: 'In all studies of existing choice programmes the evidence shows that participants have very low family incomes, predominantly come from single mother households and have a prior record of low academic performance'. They are, in many cases, the rump.

This is not a horror waiting to happen once the voucher legislation is enacted. These ineducable children are here with us today, attending (or, more likely, not attending) the sink inner-city schools Liberal Democrat and Labour MPs would transform with an injection of cash and a sprinkling of morale boosting praise. These fantasists should read Martin Johnson's brilliant account of what it is like to work in an inner-city school, *Failing School, Failing City*. Politically, Martin and I could not be further apart. We disagree profoundly over key issues such as inspection, parental choice, and, indeed, the role of the private sector. I acknowledge, however, the truth of his description. Think for a moment if you are worried by the argument that vouchers would create a two-tier system about what it is like *now* in some inner-city schools. You would not want, if you are a parent, your child educated in such a school. You are unlikely, if you are a teacher, to want to work in one:

Jason and Lance sit together at the back of the room. They are not on task. They mostly talk to each other. Occasionally they lean forward to attract the attention of Joe or Matthew, sitting in front of them, or Michelle, sitting next to them. When he thinks the teacher is not looking, Jason spits out of the open first floor window. Lance is fidgeting with felt-tip pens. He tends to break into a few lines of pop songs, in a quiet way . . .

A wasp flies through the window. Jason makes great play of swatting it, while Lance prepares a swatter by rolling up his exercise book. Lance chases the wasp round the room, joined by another boy. Gently the teacher suggests that if they leave it alone it will go away, but the chase is too exciting. Most pupils are disturbed by this but do not join in; they simply watch the action. Eventually the wasp escapes, and order is restored. The teacher continues to move from table to table, checking on progress. On reaching Jason and Lance, she firmly says she expects to see something completed by the end of the lesson. Shortly afterwards, Lance wanders round the room, apparently hoping to 'borrow' some answers, but returns to his table when instructed.

The scene is apparently calm, with a low level of noise from conversations between partners at tables, and more people working than not. As the lesson moves into its final third, however, the calm starts to be put under pressure. As the teacher moves past a table, she pushes a bag from the gangway further under the table. There is a sharp reaction from James.

'Don't touch my bag.'

'I was just pushing it out of the way.'

'Don't touch my bag, alright, just don't touch my bag.'

'James, all I did . . .'

'I said, don't touch my bag. Do I touch your handbag? Do I? Do I touch your handbag?'

'James, there's no need to talk . . .'

'Do I touch your handbag, though, do I? Do I? Do I?'

The teacher moves away, towards the other side of the room, saying, 'Don't be rude, James . . . James . . . James', and the exchange ends . . .

With five minutes to go, the class automatically moves into finishing the lesson, with little resistance from the teacher. When the bell goes, the teacher dismisses the class name by name, leaving Joe, Jason and Lance. She closes the classroom door. A girl from another group opens it from outside. The teacher closes it again. One of the other boys in the group opens it from the outside. The teacher closes it again.

'I'm going, miss', says Jason. The teacher ignores this, talking to Joe about a detention he had missed. Joe agrees to do it tonight, but as they complete the conversation Jason walks out. Joe is dismissed, and the teacher asks Lance about his work. Lance becomes discomfited, gets up, and starts to walk away. The teacher tells him that he and Jason will be separated from now on, just as Lance walks out of the room.

The teacher has stayed calm throughout. 'There's no point in getting worked up', she tells me. 'I know that if I just keep plugging away, I'll get there in the end'.

Maybe she will. Most teachers, unless they are outstandingly talented, and, it goes without saying, phenomenally committed, will not. We need a new honesty and a radically different approach. If the state could do it, then I would be happy for the state to do it. But, in general, the state has not done it. Individual schools are transformed by outstanding headteachers. Too many continue to languish.

VI

The answer? A private, for profit industry must, as Milton Friedman pointed out all those years ago, be developed in order to provide effective competition to state schools. There is now no alternative. The private sector has to be involved in the delivery of state education. Labour, as I hope I have by now demonstrated, has done everything possible to reform the state machine. It has not worked. Mr Blair, if his rhetoric is to be believed, might be beginning to recognise this, though the signs on the ground are not good. For example, the contract that Nord Anglia, a private sector for profit organisation, had to run a number of services in Hackney LEA has not been renewed. Estelle Morris has decided that a 'not for profit' trust is the better solution. On the wider political front we have, at the time of writing, the Railtrack debacle and heated controversy over whether National Health Service reform should or should not involve greater use of the private sector. The left still chokes at the prospect of fat cats profiteering from public services. The fact that the private sector supplies books and computers and equipment to schools and has done for years is conveniently forgotten; the possibility that the public might receive a better service at no greater cost ignored. It is illogical and it is knee jerk, but it is all too real: a hard core emotional resistance that will without doubt block reform unless the Prime Minister forces the pace.

I am not assuming that private sector, for profit companies will necessarily succeed or that the state and not for profit organisations will automatically fail. Everything, obviously enough, will depend on the energy and professional understanding that the particular company brings to the particular situation. Indeed, the progress that the 3 Es, a not for profit organisation, seems to have made in turning round a failed Surrey school, King's Manor, shows that in practice the for profit/not for profit distinction can be a bit of a red herring. We can argue till the cows come home about whether the profit imperative does or does not lead to greater efficiency and better results. I happen to think that, in general, it does, but, if we are looking, as we are, for a national strategy, this is not the point. Mr Blair has to be confident that the market is strong enough to deliver. He needs a significant number of reliable providers. This means swallowing the for profit pill. Ms Morris's plans to encourage successful schools to run failing schools on the side simply does not stack up as a national policy. In some cases it will work because outstanding heads make it work. But it is a cottage industry, a transparent attempt to be seen to be doing something new whilst not in reality challenging the public sector status quo. There are not enough such headteachers, and, in any case, many very good heads want nothing to do with the scheme for the obvious and understandable reason that they care too much about the schools they are, after all, paid to run.

If we want a strong, active market, it has to be a genuine private sector, for profit approach. The profits do not have to be enormous and they should not be. But they should be real. If they are not, we will not have sufficient numbers of providers and the national transformation simply will not happen.

The failure of the concept of City Technology Colleges or, in their New Labour manifestation, City Academies, is an example of the same point. Kenneth Baker wanted to transform inner-city education through a chain of privately sponsored, quasi-independent new schools. It was, in principle, a good idea. Mr Blair is pursuing the same dream and is running into the same problem. There are not enough individuals or companies that want to sponsor such colleges. Some, for admirable, altruistic reasons do; but not enough. The schools that have been established are delivering excellent results, but if we want the numbers we have to have the private sector involvement. That means two things. There must be the opportunity to make a profit and there must be a genuine freedom to deliver. Contracts that define how the day-to-day administrative details are to be managed, that expect 'partnerships' to be established with the world and his wife, or that require the company to conform with the plethora of regulations that undermine the performance of state schools will not be acceptable.

It may well be that the jump from where New Labour is to where we need to be is just too great, but, again, let's travel hopefully. The challenge is, on the one hand, to encourage potential providers to enter the market, and, on the other, to stimulate consumer demand.

The demand is there. The anger and frustration at the failure of state schools to provide a satisfactory education is deepening by the day. Middle-class parents moan at their dinner parties and either move to the right catchment area or remortgage the existing house to pay for the fees. Working-class parents have no option. They grin and they bear it. But they do so with increasing reluctance. I was genuinely shocked by the intensity of the feelings expressed at a meeting I attended of the North Islington Labour Party when a number of extremely dissatisfied parents cast scorn on teachers who were moaning about the literacy and numeracy strategies. The teachers had been complaining about the loss of professional autonomy and the marginalisation of the arts. The parents were, how shall I put it, none too sympathetic on either score. They knew, though, that they were stuck with these teachers in these schools, and they did not like it. I did not on that occasion float the idea, but, if I had, the reaction would have been ecstatic but incredulous. Vouchers? Money to pay for our kids to go to private schools? Us? Get away . . .

Well, why not? The London Oratory School achieves examination results that put many independent schools to shame on a budget that is about half of that of the average London independent day school. I have no doubt that if the voucher were to equate to the cost of educating a child in a state school, primary or secondary, plus the sum that the LEA currently top slices to fund the 'services' it provides to schools, then it would be possible for a private sector company to provide an effective education and make a profit. It would not be as large a profit as that made by many independent schools. The classes might not be that small. There would not be the frills traditionally associated with independent schools. So what? These things do not matter if there is a chance to deliver a better education and a business case that stacks up. If there is a problem, it is finding the right site, or, indeed, any site for a new inner-city school. The Government ought, therefore, to do what it has done in establishing a number of its City Academies: to shut an existing school and re-open it as a new school.

Suppose Ms Morris were to decide not to fiddle around with a charitable trust in Hackney. She could announce that she was going to shut the three poorest performing primary schools and the worst secondary school. She could, step two, consult with parents, local businesses, and representatives of the local community to establish what those who live and work in Hackney really want from their schools. And, step three, having drawn up contracts for each school that reflect the range of views expressed, she could invite the private sector to run these schools as independent, profit-making organisations.

Again, why not? It is all too easy to imagine the hundred and one legal and practical objections that the vested interests would make to any such scheme, but, if the political will was there, they could be overcome. Working-class parents would for the first time have something of a choice. The contractual arrangements governing these new, independent schools would expect significant academic improvement. If the targets were not hit, the contract would be lost. Assuming, my earlier point, that the company has the freedom to manage, there is every reason to believe that real progress will be seen. Remaining state schools, competing with the new schools, would have to improve their performance in order to survive. It would be an extremely interesting initiative that might point the way forward. Why not?

VII

I cannot think of one good reason why not. A government that was serious about education reform and the regeneration of the inner city would get on and do it. It would, in addition, acknowledge the good sense of the philanthropist Peter Lampl's initiative to make it possible for bright children from disadvantaged backgrounds to attend selective, fee-paying schools and invest public money in a very significant expansion of the scheme. Then, second, it would develop a tax credit scheme along the lines of that introduced in Arizona in 1997. And, third, it would offer parents, teachers and members of the community the chance to open charter schools of the kind that are proving so popular across America.

Peter Lampl went to Oxford from a state grammar school. He spent a number of years working in America. On his return to England he was shocked to find that entry to Oxbridge from state schools had fallen from 64 per cent in 1978 to 42 per cent in 1985. He estimated that if we rule out students from the remaining grammar schools and Church schools, comprehensives, which educate about 85 per cent of the pupil population, secure around 20 per cent of Oxbridge places. Independent schools, which educate 7 per cent of the population, achieve 47 per cent of the places. You have a thirty times better chance of studying at Oxbridge if you attend an independent school.

'The English working class has been betrayed twice in my lifetime', the sociologist Frank Musgrove wrote in 1979, 'first in the General Strike of 1926 and then forty years later when the grammar schools "went comprehensive"'. The first betrayal made, as he commented, 'perfectly good political sense: there is no great difficulty in understanding self-interest and greed. The second is more puzzling: a revolution that practically nobody wanted. The Labour Party did not abolish the great Public Schools, the obvious strongholds of upper-class privilege; with unbelievable perversity they extinguished the only serious hope of working-class parity. The remarkable social revolution of post-war socialist Britain was this: the upper classes kept their public schools; the working classes lost theirs'. Peter Lampl is trying to ensure they win them back.

His idea is very simple. He wants to make it possible for bright children to be able to attend selective fee-paying schools irrespective of the ability of their parents to pay the fees. He wants these schools to become 'centres of excellence for the talented of all backgrounds'. To demonstrate what can be achieved, the Sutton Trust, which he has established, has funded the Belvedere School in Liverpool to establish an open access policy in its senior school from September 2000. An outreach officer visits all primary schools in the catchment area, talking to teachers and parents. Children who are thought able enough and who want to go to Belvedere sit a verbal and non-verbal reasoning test and an examination in Mathematics and English. If their parents cannot afford the fees of £4,353 a year, then the Trust pays. The cost in the first year was £185,000 and will rise to £1.7 million annually over seven years.

This might seem at first sight to be a prohibitively large sum of money. Lampl's calculations are interesting. He would like to see the Government find the resources to extend his scheme to the top one hundred independent day schools. These schools win approximately a quarter of all UK school Oxbridge places and have large numbers of students going to other elite universities. Their annual fees total some £375 million. Since some parents are earning enough money to pay the full fees the cost of introducing an open access scheme along the Belvedere lines would be £220 million. Assuming savings to the state sector of say £120 million, this reduces to £100 million – which, while a lot of money, is peanuts in the context of a total educational budget of £40 billion. Pound for pound it might well, moreover, offer significantly better value for money in terms of realising the potential of gifted children from disadvantaged backgrounds than the Government's much vaunted Excellence in Cities programme, which cost £80 million in 2000–01.

The headteachers of many leading independent schools are very enthusiastic. I am certain that parents across the country would find the scheme enormously attractive. The Government, fearful, I suppose, of the doctrinaire negativity of its unreconstructed backbenchers, makes the odd, lukewarm comment on all Peter Lampl is doing and looks, with some embarrassment, in the opposite direction. It is easier, I suppose, to tinker with the system and to pretend that partnerships between independent and grammar schools and comprehensives are going to transform the world than it is to risk genuinely radical change. I just wish they would admit it.

What is needed is a genuine leap of faith: a recognition that the state does not have to own and run every school and that there is nothing morally wrong with independent education. The Prime Minister has leapt. His backbenchers have not. Forget independent education. When I debated the motion that 'The Comprehensive Ideal has Failed' with Barry Shearman at the Oxford University Student Union in the summer of 2001 the extremity of his indignation was alarming to behold. I do not expect, therefore, Mr Blair to follow Arizona's lead and introduce legislation that allows taxpayers to claim a pound for pound tax credit if they make a donation to a charitable organisation that dispenses scholarships to allow children from disadvantaged backgrounds to attend independent schools. These charitable organisations are known in Arizona as 'school tuition organisations'. Their number increased from two to fifteen in the year the legislation was passed. Despite the fact that the new law was at the time under challenge, 4,427 Arizona residents contributed $1.8 million. In the next year another eighteen school tuition organisations were established and 31,875 residents donated $13.7 million. As a result of these donations 4,000 Arizona students, mostly from disadvantaged backgrounds, have received scholarship assistance that has made it possible for them to attend the school of their choice. My guess is that it would prove an equally popular initiative in England. Your backbenchers might not like it, but why not, Mr Blair? Why not do something to give disadvantaged children the chance to benefit from the kind of education you yourself enjoyed?

A charter school is a school that is funded by the state, but which operates outside the state bureaucracy. Almost any group that is, for whatever reason, dissatisfied with state provision can apply to open a charter school, and many have. More than 2,000 such schools now exist across America. They educate half a million children and nearly 70 per cent have a waiting list equal to their enrolment. The Government might argue that City Academies are a kind of charter school. They are in the sense that they are state funded but largely autonomous institutions, but they are not, and this is a crucial difference, the result of local, grassroots demand. It is the latter aspect that interests and appeals to me. Those states in America which have passed Charter Schools legislation are trying to do what I believe we should be doing here in England: they are finding ways to put parents in the driving seat, to rescue education from the often stultifying grip of the producer interest. And they are working. 'Charter schools', Jeannie Allen, President of the Centre for Education Reform, reports, 'are creating diverse, healthy and plentiful learning opportunities for more children. Of the fifty-three national, regional and state research studies done exploring charter schools, only three have found negative effects. The rest have found positive factors, achievements recorded, satisfaction, waiting lists healthy, voluntary integration'.

This research is unlikely, however, to influence the Government. The Education Bill which was being debated in Parliament as I wrote this chapter, was heralded as a great de-regulatory step forwards. Ministers have dreamt up a new rallying cry: 'earned autonomy'. Successful schools, that is, are to be given greater freedoms. Bravo! But nobody seemed to notice that whereas the strapline back in 1997 was 'intervention in inverse proportion to success', the burden of proof now rests with the school. All schools are guilty until they can demon-strate otherwise. What, moreover, does a school have to do if it wants to be freed from some regulation or other? It has to apply to the Secretary of State who will look at the school's academic record and decide (I joke not) what she thinks of the head-teacher. The command and control mentality lives on, whatever the spin doctors would have you believe. The evolution of government thinking on faith schools is another illustration of the same mind set. Mr Blair remains constant, and good for him. He approves of faith schools. Ms Morris is now, however, not sure what she thinks. Faith schools, she says, are a good thing, but they would be better still if they had an 'inclusive' admissions policy. A faith school, Estelle, is by definition a school that educates children of a particular faith. It is 'exclusive' because parents want it to be exclusive. It is not for the Government to expect or perhaps demand faith schools to admit quotas of children from other faiths or to enter into 'partnerships' with other kinds of school. Either we believe that parents have the right to educate their children in a school of their choice or we believe that the world would be a better place if the Government told people where and to what kind of schools they must send their children. The Secretary of State is, rather predictably, confused, but her basic attitude is pretty clear: the state does know best. We are a long way from seeing charter schools spring up across the country.

VIII

The issue at stake is as simple as it is fundamental. Do we want to find ways to make state education more responsive to parental demand? Do we, in the jargon, want to empower the consumer? Do we trust parents (all parents, not just the articulate, university educated middle class) to take sensible decisions about their children's future? Or do we think that the state knows best? If you have read this far, you will know that as far as I am concerned these are rhetorical questions. The successes of state education are down to teachers and headteachers, not politicians and their bureaucrats. Conversely, many of the ills that are currently affecting the system stem from political decisions that it was obvious at the time should never have been taken. I accept, of course, that there are parents who do not give a damn and I recognise that the state may on occasion have to intervene to protect children from the consequences of parental neglect. Most parents, however, in my experience do care. They want their children to make progress at school. They worry when they do not. They can be trusted. If Mr Blair and Ms Morris disagree, they should say so. They should spell out the paternalistic assumptions upon which their policies are based. We know best.

We, aided and abetted by The Blob, can deliver best. Trust us, and be grateful. Only, of course, they do not and they cannot. Increasingly, the electorate knows this. The trust has gone, and the gratitude, as Mr Blair might discover at the next election, could be a tad underwhelming.

CHAPTER 8

Afterword

Five years ago, the Robert Clack school in Dagenham was, the headteacher, Paul Grant, told me, 'a joke'. Exam results were poor. Sixteen per cent of the pupils achieved five GCSE A*–C grades. Twenty per cent left with no qualifications at all. Bullying was rife. Drugs were peddled more or less openly. Uniform was trainers, and, if you were lucky, a tie, worn at half-mast, of course, with a big knot and an open collar. Unsurprisingly, local parents were not impressed. Underwhelmed by its pre-eminence as a place of learning and scholarship, they re-named it the Robert Crap. If you cared about your children, you moved heaven and earth to get them into another Dagenham school. Any school, it did not much matter which, as long as it was not the Robert Crap.

Now, it is the most popular school in the borough. There are five hundred applicants for the three hundred available places. Every pupil leaves with a qualification and 30 per cent manage their five A*–C grades. Every pupil wears a blazer and a tie. Trainers are banned and drugs have been banished. Behaviour is impeccable. It often is, of course, when a visiting dignitary arrives for a state tour. A good number of schools send the deputy head to recce the territory in advance, warning pupils and teachers alike that the head and his guest are about to appear. Some decide which classes are to be visited and rehearse the lesson to a level of improbable perfection. 'This is a really good lesson', I said to a boy I was sitting next to on the back row during one such visit. 'It bloody well ought to be', he replied, 'we've been practising it for weeks'. Robert Clack was not like that. On my last visit, I was taken into an assembly. We dropped in to virtually every class. We even, and in the hundreds of school visits I have made this was a first, climbed up on to the roof to observe the kids in the playground at break. 'I know', Paul said to me as we sheltered behind a pillar from a cold December wind, 'it is a bit like paint drying, but it is really important to me. It is when they are out of lessons that the trouble so often starts'. There was no trouble that breaktime. The kids stood around, eating their crisps and drinking cans of coke, chatting quietly in groups. Five or six members of staff circulated. 'They always do', Paul told me, 'I pay them, but I'm really grateful for their support. I've got some fantastic colleagues and our success is very much down to a team effort'.

A team effort: so often it is a cliché. In this case it was not. Paul had taught at Robert Clack for years before he was appointed head. He knew what it was like in the days when it was pretty well impossible for teachers to teach or children to learn. He took me into a science class to say hello to John Jarzabek, who had worked in the school for twenty-seven years. He smiled. 'I did not mean', he said, 'to stay that long. Five years, I thought, perhaps, for the experience and then, get promotion, move on. Only it did not work out like that. Somehow it seemed important, more important than going off to teach in the suburbs. Yes, it was pretty awful a while ago. Everyone believed that it was our fault. Everyone thought that if you worked at Robert Clack you must be a lousy teacher, a failure.

Most of us weren't. Most of us, in fact, were pretty good. We had to be, if we were to survive in an environment where there was no support, no . . .'. He did not want to say it. He did not want to be disloyal to his previous headteacher, but the word 'leadership' hung unspoken in the air.

As I said in my introductory chapter, the struggle to raise standards in our schools is a complex story. Here was John, an outstanding teacher who, because he had worked in a failing school, had himself been labelled a failure. Leadership matters. If there were more Paul Grants, there would be more successful teachers. If more money went into successful schools, headteachers like Paul would not have to struggle with the damp that seeps in through the flat roofs. He would not have to worry about the daily trauma of supervising nine hundred children as they move round a school built for three hundred. He could appoint (a government initiative he applauded) more 'learning mentors' to support children who are experiencing problems. But Paul, as he said repeatedly during my visit, depends absolutely upon his colleagues. 'The heads who go under', he said, 'are so often the heads who cannot win over their staff. They have to patrol the playgrounds on their own. Everything has to come from them. Not surprisingly, they get exhausted. They give up. It all becomes too much and they retreat into defeatism and cynicism'.

Defeatist, Paul is not. I asked him whether he, like so many of his colleagues, was finding it difficult to find staff. 'No, not really', he replied, 'a lot arrive at the school, see the tower blocks and wonder whether they really want to work in Dagenham. But then they come into the school. They talk to some of the kids and meet the staff and they think, "well, maybe this is the place for me"'. They stay, too. The school appointed sixteen NQTs (newly qualified teachers) last year. They are all still there. Nationally, there is a huge problem in retention. Forty per cent of student teachers do not make it to the classroom. A further 18 per cent leave the profession within three years. Not at Robert Clack. The sense of community, the certainty that if you have problems with a pupil Paul Grant and his senior management team will be there to back you up, the pleasure of being able to teach and make a difference to children who might otherwise do nothing with their lives: these things matter. 'Why don't you come and work with us?' Paul Grant asks teachers at interview. 'Why don't you share our vision? We are trying to change society.'

He is succeeding. Sadie, for example, arrived in this country from Somalia aged ten, unable to speak a word of English. She now has ten A* GCSEs. Her teachers predict that she will achieve top grades in all her A levels. She wants to read medicine at Cambridge and, having met her on a previous visit to the school, I would be amazed if she does not make it. John, a very different pupil, teetered on the edge of exclusion. His language was foul, his behaviour unpredictable. The school persevered. I chatted to him in the Learning Support Unit and congratulated him on his work. He knew he had been given a chance he could not afford to throw away and that he was very lucky to be at this particular school. My guess is that he, in his different way, will make it, too.

Paul Grant is a very unusual human being and an exception-ally gifted headteacher. Robert Clack is one of the most impressive schools I've visited. There are others, of course, like it, not enough, but an increasing number. Visiting such schools kept me going in my darker hours as Chief Inspector. Thinking about them in the weeks after I had resigned led me to write this book.

'It is a battle, Chris', Paul said to me over lunch after my tour of the school, 'a battle between good and evil'. I thought about what he meant as I stop-started my way back into London through the A13's interminable roadworks. It is a battle, obviously, against poverty and drugs and crime and the trauma and disruption of divorce. School, for many kids, is their first and last chance. But it is a battle, too, within the school: a battle to raise expectations, to deal with the children who cannot or will not conform to the norms of ordinary schooling, to support and when necessary challenge the staff, to build the right relationships with parents who are not always totally supportive or wholly reasonable, to chivvy the local authority into doing something, yet again, about the damp that is seeping through the flat roof, to juggle the hundred and one different national initiatives and keep on top of the paper mountain. Evil is too strong, perhaps, too melodramatic a word, but it comes close to capturing what I have been trying to write about in this book.

On the one hand, the daily relentless grind, the integrity and commitment of headteachers like Paul Grant and teachers like John Jarzabek. On the other the self-indulgence and irrelevance of the theorising about 'holistic problematised pedagogies', the arrogance of ministers and their officials who think they know best and who more often than not make life harder for those who actually have to deliver, the proliferation of quangos that consume millions and millions of pounds of taxpayers' money, and the hypocrisy of unions that pretend they are on the side of the children while defending, however indefensible they might be, the interests of their members.

It is a battle I tried to fight as Chief Inspector, identifying schools like Robert Clack that year by year were raising standards, and, at the other end of the spectrum, those that were failing. I tried, too, though it upset ministers and brought the wrath of the Select Committee down upon me, to point to the failures of policy and the negative impact of discredited educational ideas. It is a battle that is far from won. Indeed, while the apparatus of the state continues to dominate all that happens in our schools it will never be won. Could it be dismantled? If enough teachers were prepared to disassociate themselves from the nonsense that surrounds them and enough politicians were courageous enough to step back and think about the mistakes of the last few years, it might. It just might.

Notes

v E. D. Hirsh Junior, *The Schools We Need*, London Bantam Doubleday, 1996
Milton Friedman, Washington Post, 19 February 1995, reprinted in *An Education Agenda*, Dallas, National Center for Policy Analysis, 2001

Introduction

3 Robert Holland, 'Institutional Roadblocks to Reform', in *An Education Agenda*, National Centre for Policy Analysis, 2001
7 'Why Half of All Parents Want Pupils to go Private', *Daily Mail*, 26 October 2001

Chapter 1: Standards

12 *Standards in Public Examinations 1975–1995*, Ofsted/SCAA, 1996
14 Essays to Order for Students on the Net'. *The Times*, 8 September 2001
15 Jeffrey Robinson, 'Passmarks Lowered Throughout Decade', *Evening Standard*, 23 August 2001
17 *Knowledge and Skills for Life*, OECD, 2001

Chapter 2: The Lunacy of Learnacy

48 *Schools in the Learning Age*, Bill Lucas and Toby Greany (eds), Campaign for Learning, 2000

49 Howard Gardner, *The Unschooled Mind*, Fontana, 1993

50 Michael Barber, *The Learning Game*, Gollancz, 1996
Tim Brighouse, 'Beyond Wildest Dreams', *Times Educational Supplement*, 20 October 2000

51 David Hargreaves, *The Challenge for the Comprehensive School*, Routledge, 1982
John Macbeath, 'Turning the Tables', *Times Educational Supplement*, 22 February, 1998

52 Tom Bentley and Kimberley Seltzer, *The Creative Age*, Demos, 1999

53–56 Quotations are from Valerie Baylis, *Opening Minds: Education for the 21st Century*, RSA, 1999

57–59 *The Journal*, 21st Century Learning Initiative, June 1998

60 Letter to *Times Higher Education Supplement*, 11 June 1993

Chapter 3: Teachers and Teaching

68 David Marsland, *Towards Teacher Professionalism*, Campaign for Real Education

70 John Bangs, *The Guardian*, 16 October 2001

74 David Hargreaves, *Creative Professionalism*, Demos, 1998

75 Jonathan Smith, *The Learning Game*, Little, Brown, 2000

76 John MacBeath, Turning the Tables', *Times Educational Supplement*, 22 February, 1998

86–87 'Think Tank Report to Governing Council', National College for School Leadership

Chapter 4: OFSTED

109 Professor Carol Taylor Fitzgibbon, *Ofsted Schmofsted*, School of Education, Newcastle University

112–113 Stuart Maclure, *The Inspector's Calling*, Hodder and Stoughton, 2000

Chapter 5: Local Education Authorities

119 Christine Whatford, 'It's business as usual-LEAs are here to stay', *Times Educational Supplement*, 23 February 2001

119–22, Capital Strategies, *The Business of Education*, May 2001

132–20 '*Re-Centralization or Strategic Management?*', Centre for Educational Outreach and Innovation, Columbia University, New York

Chapter 6: Universities

136–7 John Henry Newman, 'The Idea of a University', in *Newman: Prose and Poetry*, ed Geoffey Tillotson, 1957

137 Margaret Hodge, 'Elitism never Made a Nation Rich', *Guardian*, 6 November 2001

141 Dunstan Perera, Rostrum, *Guardian*, 17 October 2000

145–146 Francis Beckett, 'Class Divisions', *The Stakeholder*

148–9 Article in *Yorkshire Post*, 21 August 2000

149 Anthony O'Hear, *The Dearing Report on Higher Education*, Centre for Policy Studies, 1997

152–3 John O'Leary, 'University entrance made easier to swell numbers', *The Times*, 27 December 2000

154 Kevin Sharpe, *The Daily Telegraph*, 14 March 2001

Chapter Seven: The Way Forward

161 Tony Storey, "So You Want to be a Teacher", May 2001

168 Departmental Report, Department for Education and Skills, March 2001

173 Geoffrey Partington, *Teacher Education in England and Wales*, IEA, 1999

174 Colin Richards, quoted in Partington, *Teacher Education in England and Wales*

183 *An Education Agenda*, published by the National Center for Policy Analysis, 2001

185 Virginia Walden, 'The Case for School Choice in Washington D. C.', in *An Education Agenda*, 98–103

187 'The Development of Private Voucher Programmes', in *An Education Agenda*, 28–35

Dan McGroarty, 'New Face of School Choice', 104–110

189–91 Martin Johnson, *Failing School, Failing City*, Charlbury, Jon Carpenter, 1999

196 Frank Musgrove, *School and the Social Order*, John Wiley and Sons, 1979